"WE DARE SAY LOVE"

Supporting Achievement in the Educational Life of Black Boys

Na'ilah Suad Nasir
Jarvis R. Givens
Christopher P. Chatmon

EDITORS

Afterwords by Tyrone C. Howard
and Pedro A. Noguera

TEACHERS COLLEGE PRESS

TEACHERS COLLEGE | COLUMBIA UNIVERSITY

NEW YORK AND LONDON

Published by Teachers College Press, 1234 Amsterdam Avenue, New York, NY 10027

Copyright © 2019 by Teachers College, Columbia University

Cover photo by Amir Siddiq. Cover design by adam b. bohannon.

Library of Congress Cataloging-in-Publication Data is available at loc.gov

ISBN 978-0-8077-6107-6 (paper)
ISBN 978-0-8077-7751-0 (ebook)

Printed on acid-free paper
Manufactured in the United States of America

26 25 24 23 22 21 20 19   8 7 6 5 4 3 2 1

MULTICULTURAL EDUCATION SERIES

James A. Banks, *Series Editor*

(continued)

Contents

Series Foreword

The litany of problems that African American males experience is institutionalized within the popular imagination, the media, and within society writ large. These problems include the ways in which Black males are harshly treated by police and the courts, disciplined disproportionately within schools, perceived by teachers as adults rather than as children and adolescents who require nurturing and caring (T. C. Howard, 2014), and victimized by the school-to-prison pipeline trajectory (Clark, 2012). This book describes the African American Male Achievement (AAMA) Initiative, which was initiated in the Oakland Public Schools in 2010. It was designed to counter and resist the dominant conceptions of African American males that are institutionalized within U. S. society and to create classrooms and schools in which they would experience innovative, empowering, affirming, and culturally responsive teaching and learning.

An important component of the AAMA initiative was the creation of all-Black, all-male manhood development classes for middle and high school students that were taught by Black male teachers. An important feature of the Manhood Development Program and its pedagogical approach is an ethic of caring and love. Caring and love were manifested in the program by creating a classroom community that had many characteristics of a family in which the teacher was viewed as a father figure; negative conceptions of Black males as hypermasculine and violent were problematized, challenged, and deconstructed; and discipline was reimagined—it became corrective but caring and compassionate. The students were also given opportunities to construct healthy and positive racial and gender identities and to challenge misogynistic notions about girls and women. Because most of the instructors viewed the students as younger versions of themselves, they were able to express and convey immense empathy, concern, and understanding. The teachers in the Manhood Development Program perceived and responded to the students as children and adolescents who needed support and nurturing rather than as threatening adults, the way African American boys are often perceived by teachers in regular classrooms. African American boys are sometimes considered menacing even when they are in kindergarten.

This compassionate and heartfelt book about how African American male teachers conceptualized and created caring and loving classrooms for Black male students can encourage teachers who teach students with other gender, cultural, and ethnic characteristics to use culturally responsive and empowering pedagogies with the increasing diversity of students within U.S. schools. The culturally responsive, caring, and loving pedagogies that are described in this timely and readable book can be adapted and used with other marginalized and minoritized groups of students. Chapter 9 describes a women's studies course in which African American girls experience challenges and possibilities in constructing positive gender and racial identities. This chapter adds an important dimension to this book because it focuses on Black girls who experience racism, sexism, and sexual harassment in schools and society.

Students in the United States are becoming increasingly diverse. However, most of the nation's teachers are White, female, and monolingual. Race and institutionalized racism are significant factors that influence and mediate the interactions of students and teachers from different ethnic, cultural, and linguistic groups (G. R. Howard, 2016; T. C. Howard, 2010; Leonardo, 2013). The growing income gap between adults (Stiglitz, 2012) as well as between youth, as described by Putnam (2015) in *Our Kids: The American Dream in Crisis*, is another significant reason why it is important to help teachers understand how race, ethnicity, and class influence student learning (Suárez-Orozco, Pimentel, & Martin, 2009).

American classrooms are experiencing the largest influx of immigrant students since the beginning of the 20th century. Approximately 12.6 million new immigrants—documented and undocumented—settled in the United States in the years from 2000 to 2016 (Zong, Batalova, & Hallock, 2018). Less than 10% came from nations in Europe. Most came from Mexico, nations in South Asia, East Asia, Latin America, the Caribbean, and Central America. Most of the immigrants to the U.S. today come from India and China, not Mexico. The influence of an increasingly diverse population on U.S. schools, colleges, and universities is and will continue to be enormous.

Schools in the United States are more diverse today than they have been since the early 1900s, when a multitude of immigrants entered the United States from Southern, Central, and Eastern Europe (C. A. M. Banks, 2005). In 2017, the National Center for Education Statistics estimated that the percentage of students from ethnic minority groups made up more than 52% of the students in prekindergarten through 12th grade in U.S. public schools, an increase from 39.2% in 2001 (National Center for Education Statistics, 2017). Language and religious diversity is also increasing in the U.S. student population. A Center for Immigration Studies publication estimated that 21.6% of Americans aged 5 and above (65.5

million) spoke a language other than English at home in 2016 (Camarota & Ziegler, 2017). This percentage has doubled since 1990, and almost tripled since 1980. The significant number of immigrants from nations such as India and China has also greatly increased religious diversity in the United States. Harvard professor Diana L. Eck (2001) calls the United States the "most religiously diverse nation on earth" (p. 4). Islam is now the fastest-growing religion in the United States, as well as in several European nations such as France, the United Kingdom, and the Netherlands (Banks, 2009; O'Brien, 2016).

The major purpose of the Multicultural Education Series is to provide preservice educators, practicing educators, graduate students, scholars, and policymakers with an interrelated and comprehensive set of books that summarizes and analyzes important research, theory, and practice related to the education of ethnic, racial, cultural, and linguistic groups in the United States and the education of mainstream students about diversity. The dimensions of multicultural education, developed by Banks (2004) and described in the *Handbook of Research on Multicultural Education* and in the *Encyclopedia of Diversity in Education* (Banks, 2012), provide the conceptual framework for the development of the publications in the series. The dimensions are content integration, the knowledge construction process, prejudice reduction, equity pedagogy, and an empowering institutional culture and social structure. The books in the Multicultural Education Series provide research, theoretical, and practical knowledge about the behaviors and learning characteristics of students of color (Conchas & Vigil, 2012; Lee, 2007), language minority students (Gándara & Hopkins 2010; Valdés, 2001; Valdés, Capitelli, & Alvarez, 2011), low-income students (Cookson, 2013; Gorski, 2013), and other minoritized population groups, such as students who speak different varieties of English (Charity Hudley & Mallinson, 2011), and LGBTQ youth (Mayo, 2014).

Other books in the Multicultural Education Series describe the problems that specific groups of students experience in schools and envision creative and practical policies and pedagogical responses. These titles include *Black Male(d): Peril and Promise in the Education of African American Males* by Tyrone C. Howard, *Streetsmart Schoolsmart: Urban Poverty and the Education of Adolescent Boys* by Gilberto Q. Conchas and James Diego Vigil, *Asians in the Ivory Tower: Dilemmas of Racial Inequality in American Higher Education* by Robert T. Teranishi, and *"To Remain an Indian": Lessons in Democracy from a Century of Native American Education* by K. Tsianina Lomawaima and Teresa L. McCarty.

I finished reading this book with hope and optimism about the Manhood Development Program that is being implemented in the Oakland Public Schools but with serious concerns about the structural problems that African American families are experiencing because of the intractable political, economic, and social problems in U.S. society. The gap between rich and poor people in the United States continues to escalate (Murray, 2012; Stiglitz, 2012) and is used by politicians to mobilize angry populist groups who embrace classism, racism, and xenophobia (Anderson, 2017). The sharp race and class divide in American society disproportionately affects African American and other families of color. Economic factors such as high rates of unemployment are a major reason why a large percentage of fathers are absent from African American families (Wilson, 1996). In a class taught by one of the teachers quoted in this book, only three of the 21 boys in his class grew up with a father in their homes.

In addition to creating innovative school programs such as the Manhood Development classes, major structural changes and reforms must take place in the political economy of the United States in order to create equal educational opportunities for African American youth and other youth who are victims of institutionalized racism, poverty, and marginalization. While school reform and the creation of innovative and transformative educational approaches such as those used in the Manhood Development Program are essential, they are not sufficient (Anyon, 1997). Major structural changes within the nation's political economy are also needed to actualize educational equality for all of the nation's youth, which will require political action (Boggs, 1998) and visionary leadership.

—James A. Banks

REFERENCES

Anderson, C. (2017). *White rage: The unspoken truth of our racial divide.* New York, NY: Bloomsbury.

Anyon, J. (1997). *Ghetto schooling: A political economy of urban educational reform.* New York, NY: Teachers College Press.

Banks, C. A. M. (2005). *Improving multicultural education: Lessons from the intergroup education movement.* New York, NY: Teachers College Press.

Banks, J. A. (2004). Multicultural education: Historical development, dimensions, and practice. In J. A. Banks & C. A. M. Banks (Eds.), *Handbook of research on multicultural education* (2nd ed., pp. 3–29). San Francisco, CA: Jossey-Bass.

Banks, J. A. (Ed.). (2009). *The Routledge international companion to multicultural education.* New York, NY and London, UK: Routledge.

Banks, J. A. (2012). Multicultural education: Dimensions of. In J. A. Banks (Ed.), *Encyclopedia of diversity in education* (vol. 3, pp. 1538–1547). Thousand Oaks, CA: Sage Publications.

Boggs, G. L. (1998). *Living for change: An autobiography.* Minneapolis, MN: University of Minnesota Press.

Camarota, S. A., & Ziegler, K. (2017, October). 65.5 million U.S. residents spoke a foreign language at home in 2016. *The Center for Immigration Studies.* Retrieved from cis.org/Report/655-Million-US-Residents-Spoke-Foreign -Language-Home-2016

Charity Hudley, A. H., & Mallinson, C. (2011). *Understanding language variation in U.S. schools.* New York, NY: Teachers College Press.

Clark, C. (2012). School-to-prison pipeline. In J. A. Banks (Ed.), *Encyclopedia of diversity in education* (Vol. 4, pp. 1894–1897). Thousand Oaks, CA: Sage.

Conchas, G. Q., & Vigil, J. D. (2012). *Streetsmart schoolsmart: Urban poverty and the education of adolescent boys.* New York, NY: Teachers College Press.

Cookson, P. W., Jr. (2013). *Class rules: Exposing inequality in American high schools.* New York, NY: Teachers College Press.

Eck, D. L. (2001). *A new religious America: How a "Christian country" has become the world's most religiously diverse nation.* New York, NY: HarperSanFrancisco.

Gándara, P., & Hopkins, M. (Eds.). (2010). *Forbidden language: English language learners and restrictive language policies.* New York, NY: Teachers College Press.

Gorski, P. C. (2013). *Reaching and teaching students in poverty: Strategies for erasing the opportunity gap.* New York, NY: Teachers College Press.

Howard, G. R. (2016). *We can't teach what we don't know: White teachers, multiracial schools* (3rd ed.). New York, NY: Teachers College Press.

Howard, T. C. (2010). *Why race and culture matter in schools. Closing the achievement gap in America's classrooms.* New York, NY: Teachers College Press.

Howard, T. C. (2014). *Black male(d): Peril and promise in the education of African American males.* New York, NY: Teachers College Press.

Lee, C. D. (2007). *Culture, literacy, and learning: Taking bloom in the midst of the whirlwind.* New York, NY: Teachers College Press.

Leonardo, Z. (2013). *Race frameworks: A multidimensional theory of racism and education.* New York, NY: Teachers College Press.

Lomawaima, K. T., & McCarty, T. L. (2006). *"To remain an Indian:" Lessons in democracy from a century of Native American education.* New York, NY: Teachers College Press.

Mayo, C. (2014). *LGBTQ youth and education: Policies and practices.* New York, NY: Teachers College Press.

Murray, C. (2012). *Coming apart: The state of White America, 1960–2010.* New York, NY: Crown Forum.

National Center for Education Statistics. (2017). *Enrollment and percentage distribution of enrollment in public elementary and secondary schools, by race/ethnicity and region: Selected years, fall 1995 through fall 2025.* Retrieved from nces.ed.gov/programs/digest/d15/tables/dt15_203.50.asp

O'Brien, P. (2016). *The Muslim question in Europe: Political controversies and public philosophies.* Philadelphia, PA: Temple University Press.

Putnam, R. D. (2015). *Our kids: The American dream in crisis.* New York, NY: Simon & Schuster.

Stiglitz, J. E. (2012). *The price of inequality: How today's divided society endangers our future.* New York, NY: Norton.

Suárez-Orozco, C., Pimentel, A., & Martin, M. (2009). The significance of relationships: Academic engagement and achievement among newcomer immigrant youth. *Teachers College Record, 111*(3), 712–749.

Teranishi, R. T. (2010). *Asians in the ivory tower: Dilemmas of racial inequality in American higher education.* New York, NY: Teachers College Press.

Valdés, G. (2001). *Learning and not learning English: Latino students in American schools.* New York, NY: Teachers College Press.

Valdés, G., Capitelli, S., & Alvarez, L. (2011). *Latino children learning English: Steps in the journey.* New York, NY: Teachers College Press.

Wilson, W. J. (1996). *When work disappears: The world of the new urban poor.* New York, NY: Knopf.

Zong, J., Batalova, J., & Hallock, J. (2018, February). *Frequently requested statistics on immigrants and immigration in the United States.* Migration Policy Institute. Retrieved from www.migrationpolicy.org/article/frequently -requested-statistics-immigrants-and-immigration-united-states#Demographic

CHAPTER 1

We Dare Say Love

Black Male Student Experiences and the Possibilities Therein

Jarvis R. Givens and Na'ilah Suad Nasir

"Gimme hate, Lord," he whimpered. "I'll take hate any day. But don't give me love. I can't take no more love, Lord. I can't carry it. . . . It's too heavy. Jesus, you know, you know all about it. Ain't it heavy? Jesus? Ain't love heavy?"

—Henry Porter, character from Toni Morrison's (1977) *Song of Solomon*

It seems that America has tolerated and grown accustomed to the under-education of African American males largely because it has written this off as a "black problem." Rather than being embraced as an American problem and challenge, our leaders in politics, business and education, have implored the Black community to do something, while washing their hands of responsibility for the failure of public institutions that should serve them.

—Pedro Noguera (2015)

Love is tricky business in a world that confines you with hate, even before your name has been given as song to air. Henry Porter insinuates this, while in a drunken fit, during the opening scene of Toni Morrison's novel *Song of Solomon*. The costs of love are formidable, he surmises. When hate is the only register one knows the world to speak from, the costs of love are debatably too much to bear. It requires a disarming, the removing of masks used for protection while navigating hostile terrain. It requires trust and vulnerability in the same world that has condemned you. This hate is lived history for Black males. It makes it hard to take stock in fleeting pronouncements of love, or acts of good faith from people and places you have come to distrust. Even with those who genuinely invoke love and care, this can be difficult, especially if you are convinced that even *their* love has no power to truly protect you.

1

More central to the discussion in this book—society and the schools embedded within it have made love a foreign thing for Black males. It has become difficult to comprehend a sincere relationship between public schools and Black male students (or all Black children for that matter) that is predicated on love. The American school, with few exceptions, is too often the place where Black students come to know that they are despised, feared, and deemed to be of little to no human value in the world. In this context, the gamble of love is high stakes. Yet those who care deeply for Black children, as extensions of ourselves, recognize that insisting on love anyhow is of the first order.

America has proven itself to be well adjusted to Black suffering (Dumas, 2014), and particularly so for African American males. Not only is it well adjusted, but the public imagination has narrated this suffering as a problem of Black people's own doing and their failure to assimilate to "normative" culture. In no space is this more evident than in the American school, with (perhaps) the exception of prisons. Yet, as scholarship has increasingly shown, these two societal institutions are closely linked in their relationship to the precarious position of African Americans. The reality of Black male students makes this strikingly clear. Through a dynamic interplay of low expectations, anxieties around Black male criminality, and racialized educational tracking, Black boys are pushed out of schools and into prisons at alarming rates. In fact, the carceral experiences of African American males begin as early as elementary school through a perverse system of disciplinary practices, where these young men are punished more than any other group in American schools (Schott Foundation for Public Education, 2015). While the convenient response is to ask, "What's wrong with these students?" an abundance of scholarship has demonstrated how and why this peculiar crisis in education is largely attributed to structural forms of inequality, anti-Black sentiments of educators, and widely held perceptions that African American boys are less capable and more in need of discipline than their peers. Racist and gendered ideas have historically shaped school practices, and the positionality of Black boys has historically made them uniquely vulnerable within this societal institution. This is the state of affairs.

Black male students have been confined by a life of death and dying in American society. A common narrative suggests Black males are lucky to live to see the age of 25; such storylines relegate these youth to a perturbed psychic reality. This is particularly apparent in a moment when spectacular images of Black male death have become so visually pervasive. The viral images of Black men and boys being killed by police or dehumanized in various carceral contexts have produced a present-day national memory of state-sanctioned Black male death. This memory is not new, but the resurgence of these images—and the reality of them—fortify ideas offered to Black male youth, suggesting that their lives are immediately confined by fatality, even as they strive toward living.

This book is concerned with a school-focused, districtwide initiative created for African American male students by Black community members, educators, and district officials in Oakland, California, to combat the mechanisms by which schools and society continue to diminish the life chances of Black boys. The African American Male Achievement (AAMA) Initiative in Oakland dared to center love and the notion of Black male educational success, amidst a societal moment that reproduced Black male suffering in the streets and in the classrooms. In 2010, the leaders of this initiative, many of whom were African American parents as well as educators, argued that to be effective, they must utilize an asset-based approach. They set out to work with Black male students, whom they understood to be constantly in pursuit of life instead of death, despite the circumstances they faced. This book tells the story of the institutional and pedagogical development of AAMA and its innovative programming.

The work being done through AAMA emerged as cutting-edge not simply because of its specific focus on Black boys, but also because it was a districtwide effort that drew funding from within but also outside of the district. This was not a program on the outskirts of schooling. It became integrated during the school day, in after-school settings, and at the table of district leadership, and it manifested in strategic partnerships with parents, community leaders and organizations, and Black male educators.

While other transformative work has addressed the challenges faced by African American male students, it is often taken up by community organizations, or through individual programs or school sites. This is to say, school districts often fail to recognize or purposefully acknowledge their role in the contentious schooling experiences of Black male students. The AAMA initiative demonstrates awareness on the part of district leadership that there are very real issues of structural oppression that exist within the organizational contexts of schools, and in a district's stride toward addressing it within its infrastructure. This is an important step toward recognizing that when it comes to the "achievement gap" (better stated as an "educational debt" [Ladson-Billings, 2006]), the issues do not rest solely with individuals; these are structural and institutional patterns. This institutional recognition pushes back against the deficit narrative that has posed great challenges to the schooling experiences of historically marginalized children, and Black boys in particular. The creation of AAMA on the part of Oakland Unified School District (OUSD) was a bold step forward—though not without its challenges.

AFRICAN AMERICAN MALES AND SCHOOL

The raced and gendered experience of Black males requires a dynamic analytical perspective to both honor and interrogate their lived realities. Attending only to the race or gender component of their experiences would obscure their positionality in the broader society. While White boys may be privileged because of their male gender in society, Black boys (as it has historically been the case) are vulnerable in unique ways because of where they stand in relation to White supremacy and patriarchy. Attending to Black boys' schooling experiences requires that we be attuned to how Blackness and maleness interact in unique ways, both in terms of Black male students' identity development, and also with respect to how Black males and their actions are often interpreted in school contexts (Curry, 2017; Givens, 2016; Nasir et al., 2013). The racial story lines that shape public perceptions of Black males present them as the ultimate menace to society—criminal from birth, ignorant, violent, and predatorily hypersexual. These ideas, unfortunately, come to inform practice and shape experience. Because of this, Black males are particularly vulnerable to certain forms of racialized violence and neglect because of their intersectional identities as Black and male (and often poor), not because of one or the other. The implications of this are evidenced by their experience with discipline, low enrollment in AP courses, reading and math proficiency rates, and low graduation rates. It is also evident in their testimonies about how they experience schooling and various forms of aggressive neglect in educational structures.

Negative schooling statistics are reflective of structured patterns of neglect and violence, not of Black males' lack of capacity. A flowering of scholarship has identified Black males performing at high academic levels, particularly when they have appropriate social–emotional support and experience affirming environments (Howard, Douglas, & Warren, 2016; Warren, 2017). These stories are an anomaly to most schools, because the norms of the American school continue to be informed by dominant forms of power and social relations. Thus, it is no coincidence that racial trends in the world of prisons mirror what happens in schools (Rios, 1994; Shedd, 2015; Sojoyner, 2016), for we know schools are nodes of our larger society.

In 2015, the Schott Foundation released its biannual report on Black males and education as a sort of national report card. The findings were not good news. With respect to discipline, 15% of Black male students received out-of-school suspension compared to 7% and 5% for their Latino and White male counterparts, respectively (Schott Foundation for Public Education, 2015, p. 34). National high school graduation rates were reported to be 59% for Black males, 69% for Latino males, and 80% for

White males. When we turn to 8th-grade Black male math and reading proficiency rates for the 2013 year, 12% were proficient in reading and 13% in math, in comparison to 17% and 21% for Latino males, and 38% and 45% for White males. Relatedly, few African American males have access to advanced and academically rigorous courses in high school, thus diminishing their chances of college readiness. Only 7.6% of Black males were enrolled in Advanced Placement classes compared to 18.4% of White males (Schott Foundation for Public Education, 2015, pp. 7, 37, 42).

To be clear, anti-Blackness in the American school disproportionately impacts both African American boys and girls. As Kimberlé Crenshaw has shown, Black girls experience school discipline in an egregious disproportion compared to their White counterparts. For instance, in the city of New York during the 2013–2014 school year, there were 13,823 cases of disciplining Black boys and 9,076 cases of disciplining Black girls. This meant 57% of all male disciplinary cases were Black boys, and 61% of all female disciplinary cases were Black girls. Black students made up 28% of the student population (Crenshaw, Ocen, & Nanda, 2015, pp. 18–19). Thus, Black students (boys and girls) were grossly overpunished in schools, and this is particularly the case for Black males when we look at the sheer number of cases. These trends of racialized disproportionality in school discipline are an extension of a larger history in which social institutions premised on public good and citizenship ideals have rendered Black youth as undeserving and untenable as innocent children—as not fully human (Bernstein, 2011; Dumas & Nelson, 2016; Ward, 2015).

Research on the experiences of Black male students in school has attended to multiple aspects of schooling. Scholars have worked to name structural apparatuses that impede on Black male success. Others focus on the interpersonal aspects of schooling. Some researchers even look to the personal motivations of these students to make sense of their educational experiences (see Dumas, 2016; Ferguson, 2001; Howard & Associates, 2017; Johnson, Pate, & Givens, 2010; Nasir et al., 2013; Noguera, 2003; Rios, 1994; Warren, 2017).

The best of this scholarship raises a necessary caution against any educational strategies for Black males that focus solely on personal decisionmaking and behavioral development. Such interventions often move toward suggesting that Black males are the problem (rather than larger structural phenomena such as poverty, high unemployment, lack of health care, school tracking, and the prison–industrial complex). As Michael Dumas has acutely noted (2016, p. 97), many of these programs, which are "arguably beneficial," are "being advanced within a neoliberal project intended to undermine more fundamental change by locating problems within (the bodies) of Black boys and young men rather than in the social and economic order." These interventions often advocate for people and communities to "take responsibility" for their actions in a way that distorts how many of the challenges African American males and their communities face are results of racialized aggressive neglect on the part of the state. In short, the behaviors of Black boys are not the root of the problem. The root of the problem can only be located in structural practices that create the conditions in particular communities, and the perpetual lack of public interest in addressing rank inequality, especially when it comes to Black people. Yet Black children continue to be "adultified" in school settings— perceived as smaller versions of the terrifying, criminal, pathological adults they are expected to become (Ferguson, 2001). They are barred from childhood and perceived to be more in need of harsh punishment, unwilling to learn, or simply ineducable altogether.

We do not intend to suggest that it is useless to engage in identity and sociobehavioral work with Black male students or that educational strategy should focus solely on structure. As Pedro Noguera has pointed out, we must work to engage both structural and cultural approaches. There is a need to synthesize both structural and cultural explanations of human behavior to best support Black students. "Structural and cultural forces combine in complex ways to influence the formation of individual and collective identities, even as individuals may resist, actively or passively, the various processes involved in the molding of the 'self'" (2003, p. 442). We must value the voices of Black students, hear how they articulate their experiences, and empower them with strategies and more expansive ideas of how they can exist and function in their environments, even as we support them in critiquing structures of domination and power (Howard & Associates, 2017). This is not locating the problem within Black male students, it is an effort to name the problem that we know they are up against and support them in navigating these challenges in healthy and developmentally appropriate ways. This must be done alongside fierce, explicit criticism of things like White supremacy, police violence, and the limited portrayals of Black masculinity via patriarchal societal norms.

Identity work for Black students must be done in critique of, and alongside efforts to change, structural practices that perpetuate racist violence and oppression. It is necessary to make these critiques of structure explicit and offer them up in a language available to students. This foundational premise—that the problem does not reside in the Black students or with their decisions—must be made with unrelenting clarity, especially when the world so deafeningly says otherwise.

Relationships between Black students and their teachers are also key for understanding their experiences in school. Student success often hinges on the strength of relationships they are able to cultivate with teachers, who become mentors and advocates (Irvine, 1988). Unfortunately, in the contemporary moment, Black students (especially Black males) continue to have poor relationships with their teachers. For instance, when 537 students at a Northern California high school were asked to respond to the claim "My teachers support me and care about my success in their class," Black males were the least likely to agree. About 80% of the Black male respondents ($n = 100$) responded with "disagree" or "strongly disagree" (Noguera, 2003, p. 448). Black males and then Black females were the least likely to agree with the claim that their teachers cared about their academic success. Sadly, this figure is likely not shocking to the readers of this book. By and large, Black male students are unfairly labeled as troublemakers and treated with little care or empathy. What's more, these negative interactions have adverse effects on Black male students' attitudes and behaviors (Dance, 2002; Ferguson, 2001; Noguera, 2009.

The poor relationships between Black students and their teachers are likely connected to the gross overrepresentation of White teachers at 82% and the underrepresentation of Black teachers at 7% of the profession (King, McIntosh, & Bell-Ellwanger, 2016). Studies have shown that significant numbers of White teachers hold bias toward Black students (Ferguson, 2001; Griffith & London, 1980; Grissom & Redding, 2016). For instance, in a 1979 study of 270 Black and White teachers in majority-minority urban schools, Griffith and London found that 64.6% of Black teachers rated their students to be of average or better ability; in contrast, 66.1% of White teachers rated these same students as average or below. In a more recent study in 2016, scholars Grissom and Redding highlighted that Black teachers are more likely than White teachers to recommend high-achieving Black students for gifted programs.

A number of scholars have reminded us that not all Black male students are underachieving and that some educational programs have done well by African American boys (Howard & Associates, 2017; Howard, Douglas, & Warren, 2016; Warren, 2017). It is important to note this as a means to demonstrate that Black male student achievement is not impossible, even in the context of a society organized to perpetuate inequality. Tyrone Howard (Howard & Associates, 2017) has encouraged us to seek out experiences of Black male students who are doing well to identify what resources were made available to them that other Black male students may not have access to. The successful students in his study described the critical role of teachers who supported them as mentors, organizations that provided social–emotional support, classroom cultures that tied material to their lived experiences, and access to an academic culture that actively cultivated a vision of Black male student success. Other scholars have expressed the demand for teachers who support Black male students, who help them make sense of their lived realities, and who create environments where they are cared for and viewed as children (Ginwright, 2010; McKinney de Royston et al., 2017). In short, schools must actively cultivate a culture of success that engages the identities of Black male students, as opposed to defining a culture of success over and against their demographic, as many currently do.

However, there remain very few models in the research literature of what it looks like when public schools take this commitment seriously. This volume takes up that challenge by presenting research findings and reflections from program leaders, instructors, and students from the African American Male Achievement Initiative in Oakland, California.

BOOK OVERVIEW

This edited volume is a case study (Yin, 2013) of the African American Male Achievement Initiative—its programs, processes, and impacts. The case study of AAMA in Oakland provides important insight for teachers, parents, community organizers, and school districts across the country about intentional practices for supporting African American males as Black boys *and* students. While this book focuses on the AAMA initiative in Oakland, its implications are potentially broad reaching. The chapters in this volume reveal a host of successes and challenges that offer insight to those engaging in similar efforts in school districts and cities across the country, and for those who study targeted educational practices for particular groups of students. The AAMA platform in Oakland emerged before President Obama's targeted action through the "My Brother's Keeper" Initiative (MBK), which established Black male achievement as a high-profile, and widely debated, national issue. Since Obama's initiative, however, many other school districts have worked to develop similar models of programming that target Black (and Brown) male students. To this end, much can be learned from Oakland's AAMA, which was the first of its kind nationally.

In 2010, the Oakland Unified School District took a targeted approach to addressing challenges faced by Black male students when they launched the Office of African American Male Achievement. This edited volume explores the work of AAMA as an example of the targeted reform practices springing up in many cities across the nation to address the educational disparities faced by Black boys, who are perceived to be the most "at risk." In Oakland, AAMA has involved stakeholders at all levels: students, community activists, district officials, research scholars, and teachers. One of the major programmatic thrusts of this office has been the creation of all-Black, all-male manhood development classes for middle and high school students across the district, taught by Black male instructors.

This book describes how AAMA, as a districtwide initiative, has worked to make equitable education more accessible to Black male students in Oakland. The volume includes chapters on the history of the initiative, the programs and practices of AAMA, and analyses of aspects of the Manhood Development Program and its pedagogical approach. It also explores the unique model of teacher recruitment and training of AAMA. Many of the chapters directly engage the voices of program instructors and AAMA staff. In doing so, the text brings into clear view the broader context of the key educational issues facing Black male students and the complex set of processes and institutional structures necessary to better support their academic achievement and well-being.

The book offers no definitive solution for reconciling the tensions of peril and promise that characterize Black male schooling experiences across the nation. It is an effort to unveil the work of a group of people committed to addressing this issue through cultivated partnerships between district administrators and grassroots organizations, youth leaders and parents, students and teachers. In raising these multiple perspectives to tell the story of AAMA, we expose many of the challenges that come with doing this work; at the same time, we highlight the innovative strategies and collaborations this team employed to overcome and adapt to many of those challenges. This book presumes that there is no one solution to addressing the crisis being faced by Black students (male or female) in our public education system. However, any practices or policies that are going to impact the hearts and minds of these students must: 1) explicitly acknowledge the past failures of schools to meet the needs of Black male students; 2) attend to the social–emotional trauma experienced by Black male students (which extends beyond school); 3) make an unyielding commitment to care about them in ways that validate their experiences; and 4) be willing to construct unconventional structures of support to meet the needs of Black male students based on their needs as children and as a distinct group of learners. These are all tenets employed in the work of AAMA.

This volume is comprised of 10 chapters and two afterwords, including several reflections from administrators and teachers inside of AAMA, and from scholars in the field. In Chapter 2, Shawn Ginwright, Christopher P. Chatmon, and Gregory Hodge provide background and context to AAMA as a race- and gender-based initiative, detailing the history of such work on behalf of Black students in Oakland, as well as some of the tensions and controversy surrounding the initiative. In Chapter 3, Na'ilah Suad Nasir and Jarvis R. Givens draw on a study of AAMA to describe a critical component of the initiative—instruction in the Manhood Development Program classrooms.[1] They highlight the importance of a love-centered pedagogical approach, and how that manifests in relation to teaching strategies, classroom community, and the upending of normative practices of school discipline. In Chapter 4, curriculum developer

Baayan Bakari reflects on the philosophy and guiding principles behind the curricular approach, and he describes the accredited classes developed under AAMA for the district. In Chapter 5, Maxine McKinney de Royston and Sepehr Vakil dive deeper into the motivations and philosophies of the instructors themselves, highlighting how the instructors saw their work as about nurturing young people, but also as political in its own right. In Chapter 6, Jahi reflects on his multiple roles in the program, including as an instructor, then later as an assistant program director. In Chapter 7, Patrick Johnson and David Philoxene identify an important caution—the perils of perpetuating narratives of damage for Black boys. Chapter 8, by Executive Director Jerome Gourdine, details the ways that AAMA approached recruiting and retaining Black male instructors. In Chapter 9, kihana miraya ross explores a parallel experience for Black girls in the district, by examining a course for Black girls run in one of the district high schools. In doing so, she also examines the possibilities and tensions in race- and gender-focused approaches. Chapter 10 shares excerpts from an interview with the founding director, Christopher Chatmon, and offers some reflections on the journey of creating AAMA, and on some of the challenges and lessons learned in that journey. The volume ends with reflections from two key scholars of Black male education, Tyrone Howard and Pedro Noguera.

NOTES

1. All instructor and student names referencing Manhood Development Program class sessions are pseudonyms.

REFERENCES

Bernstein, R. (2011). *Racial innocence: Performing American childhood from slavery to civil rights*. New York, NY: NYU Press.

Crenshaw, K., Ocen, P., & Nanda, J. (2015). *Black girls matter: Pushed out, overpoliced, and underprotected*. New York, NY: African American Policy Forum, Center for Intersectionality and Social Policy Studies. Retrieved from www .law.columbia.edu/sites/default/files/legacy/files/public_affairs/2015/february _2015/black_girls_matter_report_2.4.15.pdf

Curry, T. J. (2017). *The man-not: Race, class, genre, and the dilemmas of Black manhood*. Philadelphia, PA: Temple University Press.

Dance, L. J. (2002). *Tough fronts: The impact of street culture on schooling*. New York, NY: Routledge.

Dumas, M. J. (2014). "Losing an arm": Schooling as a site of Black suffering. *Race Ethnicity and Education, 17*(1), 1–29.

Dumas, M. J. (2016). My brother as "problem": Neoliberal governmentality and interventions for Black young men and boys. *Educational Policy, 30*(1), 94–113.

Dumas, M. J., & Nelson, J. (2016). (Re)Imagining Black boyhood: Toward a critical framework for educational research. *Harvard Educational Review, 86*(1), 537–557.

Ferguson, A. A. (2001). *Bad boys: Public schools in the making of Black masculinity* (Reprint ed.). Ann Arbor, MI: University of Michigan Press.

Ginwright, S. A. (2010). *Black youth rising: Activism & radical healing in urban America.* New York, NY: Teachers College Press.

Givens, J. R. (2016). Modeling manhood: Reimagining Black male identities in school. *Anthropology & Education Quarterly, 47*(2), 167–185.

Griffith, A. R., & London, C. B. G. (1980). Student relations among inner city teachers: A comparative study by teacher race. *Education 101*(2), 139–47.

Grissom, J. A., & Redding, C. (2016). Discretion and disproportionality: Explaining the underrepresentation of high-achieving students of color in gifted programs. *AERA Open 2*(1), 1–25.

Howard, T. C., & Associates (2017). *The counter narrative: Reframing success of high achieving Black and Latino males in Los Angeles County.* Los Angeles: University of California, Los Angeles, UCLA Black Male Institute. Retrieved from www.issuelab.org/resources/26073/26073.pdf

Howard, T. C., Douglas, T. M. O., & Warren, C. A. (2016). "What works": Recommendations on improving academic experiences and outcomes for Black males. *Teachers College Record, 118*(6). Retrieved from www.tcrecord.org/library/Issue.asp?volyear=2016&number=6&volume=118

Irvine, J. J. (1988). An analysis of the problem of disappearing Black educators. *The Elementary School Journal, 88*(5), 507.

Johnson, W., Pate, D., & Givens, J. (2010) Big boys don't cry, Black boys don't feel: The intersection of shame and worry on community violence and the social construction of masculinity among urban African American males—The case of Derrion Albert. In C. Edley Jr. & J. Ruiz de Velasco (Eds.), *Changing places: How communities will improve the health of boys of color* (pp. 462–492). Berkeley, CA: University of California Press.

King, J. B., Jr., McIntosh, A., & Bell-Ellwanger, J. (2016). *The state of racial diversity in the educator workforce.* Washington, DC: U.S. Department of Education. Retrieved from www2.ed.gov/rschstat/eval/highered/racial-diversity/state-racial-diversity-workforce.pdf

Ladson-Billings, G. (2006). From the achievement gap to the education debt: Understanding achievement in U.S. schools. *Educational Researcher, 35*(7), 3–12.

McKinney de Royston, M., Vakil, S., Nasir, N. S., ross, k. m., Givens, J., & Holman, A. (2017). "He's more like a 'brother' than a teacher": Politicized caring in a program for African American males. *Teachers College Record, 119*(4), 1–40.

Nasir, N. S., ross, k. m., McKinney de Royston, M., Givens, J., & Bryant, J. N. (2013). Dirt on my record: Rethinking disciplinary practices in an all-Black, all-male alternative class. *Harvard Educational Review, 83*(3), 489–512.

Noguera, P. A. (2003). The trouble with Black boys. *Urban Education, 38*(4), 431–459.

Noguera, P. (2009). *The trouble with Black boys: . . . And other reflections on race, equity, and the future of public education.* San Francisco, CA: Jossey-Bass.

Rios, V. (1994). *Punished: Policing the lives of Black and Latino boys.* New York, NY: NYU Press.

Schott Foundation for Public Education. (2015). *Black lives matter: The Schott 50 state report on public education and Black males.* New York, NY: The Metropolitan Center for Research on Equity and the Transformation of Schools at New York University.

Shedd, C. (2015). *Unequal city: Race, schools, and perceptions of injustice.* New York, NY: Russell Sage Foundation.

Sojoyner, D. M. (2016). *First strike: Educational enclosures in Black Los Angeles.* Minneapolis, MN: University of Minnesota Press.

Ward, G. K. (2015). *The Black child-savers: Racial democracy and juvenile justice.* Chicago, IL: University of Chicago Press.

Warren, C. A. (2017). *Urban preparation: Young Black men moving from Chicago's South Side to success in higher education.* Cambridge, MA: Harvard Education Press.

Yin, R. K. (2013). *Case study research: Design and methods* (5th ed.). Los Angeles, CA: SAGE.,

The Roots and Routes of Oakland's African American Male Achievement Initiative (AAMA)

Shawn Ginwright, Christopher P. Chatmon, and Gregory Hodge

For decades, Oakland, California, has been the epicenter of tectonic shifts in efforts to improve the educational and life outcomes for African American young men. The residents of this community have been at the forefront of national and local efforts to reverse negative trends as they pertain to this group of youth—trends we know all too well. African American boys and young men in Oakland, as well as in other urban communities around the nation, face a number of obstacles to educational success, economic mobility, and well-being (Littles, Bowers, & Gilmer, 2008; Noguera, 2009; Young, 2003). Structural barriers including poor-quality schools and fewer job opportunities have limited the life chances for Black males in comparison to their White counterparts. These barriers are sometimes justified by negative perceptions held by White employers, police, and teachers, and are often based on the fear that Black men are dangerous and a threat to public safety (Wilson, 1996). Extensive research has shown how sentencing laws, policing practices, and public policy have all contributed to disproportionate numbers of incarcerated and adjudicated Black men (Brunson & Miller, 2006; Mincy, 2006; Young, 2003). Scholars have also illustrated how film, television news, and even social science research have portrayed young Black males in ways that reinforce negative perceptions in the minds of policy stakeholders (Hutchinson, 1994). Images of young Black men have "a way of maintaining themselves in the public's mind and in the absence of quality information and analyses, these images have become the primary prisms through which people construct an understanding of social reality" (Sánchez-Jankowski, 1991, p. 302).

In Oakland, zero tolerance policies in schools, suspensions/expulsions, policing practices, and public policy have all contributed to disproportionate numbers of Black young men being disconnected from school, and exposed to risky behavior (Bryant, 2013; Edley & Ruiz de Velasco, 2010; Phillips & Bryant, 2013). These challenges become more difficult for African American boys and young men to cope with given their bombardment with toxic messages such as "big boys don't cry" reinforced by toxic hypermasculinities that erode their ability to express themselves (Johnson, Pate, & Givens, 2010). It is within this context that efforts to improve educational outcomes for African American boys in Oakland have taken root.

Efforts to improve the outcomes for African American families in general, and young people in particular, have a long, rich, and powerful history in Oakland. In fact, these efforts in many ways are a reflection of Oakland residents' rich history of Black activism, collective power, and courageous vision for the future of Black children.

Oakland enjoys a long and rich history of activism, community engagement, and innovative solutions that address the needs of African American children. It is from this rich legacy in Oakland that AAMA found its roots. This chapter identifies a lineage of race- and gender-specific projects in Oakland prior to the African American Male Achievement program in 2010 as the critical local context that made AAMA possible and informed its strategies. It also chronicles how AAMA emerged in Oakland Unified School District, and the role community residents played in supporting the project. The chapter concludes by highlighting key programmatic components of AAMA, while also explaining how and why each of these features was created. These include the Manhood Development Program, Family Literacy Nights, and various resources provided to students and parents that attended to the social–emotional needs of Black male students.

THREE WAVES OF EFFORTS TO SUPPORT BLACK BOYS IN OAKLAND

There have been three waves of community-driven efforts directed toward addressing the academic and social needs of African American young men in Oakland. In describing these three waves, we provide broad strokes, rather than detailed accounts, of the landscape of efforts and activities in Oakland that preceded AAMA. While these waves are not exhaustive, we attempt to convey the most significant trends and activities that ultimately shaped the emergence of AAMA in Oakland.

Wave #1: Black Activism, 1960–1975

Oakland's Black political climate during the 1960s provides an important backdrop for understanding efforts to support African American youth in Oakland. During the 15-year period of 1960 to 1975, a broad constellation of political and economic opportunities existed for youth in Oakland.

These opportunities contributed to a shared sense of political optimism and a sense that change was possible. This optimism had a profound impact on the political consciousness among Oakland's Black youth and encouraged their involvement with a variety of organizations, ideas, and networks of young activists. The availability of jobs, active involvement in civic affairs, a robust parks and recreation system that notably employed and trained neighborhood youth—all made it possible for youth to later use their skills toward activism and community change. These dynamics created a culture of activism and fostered a vibrant civic life for Black youth in Oakland (Crouchett, Bunch, & Winnacker, 1989; Self, 2003). This environment also incubated new ideas about justice, birthed the Black Panther Party, and ushered in a new vision of education and schooling for African American young people.

During this period, Oakland witnessed the opening of its first Black independent schools, which focused on the holistic needs of African American children. Rooted in culture, community, and excellence, these schools served as alternatives to public schools, which ultimately failed to focus on the unique needs of Black children and their families (Ginwright, 2000). Black independent schools offered a counternarrative, one that affirmed and celebrated Black identity and culture (Rickford, 2016). San Francisco State University college students also envisioned, demanded, and created the first Black Studies department in the country (Gitlin, 1969; McEvoy & Miller, 1969). Oakland's culture of activism, community engagement, and vision of how to reform schooling for Black students resulted in powerful strategies directed at supporting Black students (Ginwright, 2004). Similarly, through its numerous community programs, free breakfast, community school, free clothing, community clinics, and grocery giveaways the Black Panther Party focused on self-determination by meeting the needs of African American families. Oakland residents had ushered in a renewed political awareness about the significance self-determination and creating education alternatives specific to the needs of African American youth conferred.

Any review of educational reform efforts in Oakland focused on race and gender would be remiss not to mention the important though short-lived career of Dr. Marcus Foster as Oakland Unified School District's first African American superintendent. Dr. Foster was hired by the school board in 1970 after protests led by the Oakland Five[1] forced the issue; he entered the scene with a range of professional education experiences from Philadelphia that prepared him for this task at the epicenter of the Black Power movement. Though generally a political moderate, Foster brought an emboldened passion for Black children and what he knew was possible for them in the city's schools. Foster was a proponent of broad community engagement and school accountability and was influenced by the radicalism of the Black Panther Party as well as by private-sector business interests. Once, at a conference titled "Telling It Like It Is," Foster was quoted as telling the assembled participants, "You'd better do something soon. Put your actions where your mouth is" (Spencer, 2012). An assassin's bullet took Foster's life on November 6, 1973, but the dream of full educational equity for Black children served by OUSD persisted.

Wave #2: African Centered Education & Rites of Passage, 1975–1990

The second wave of the race-based strategies in Oakland can best be described as African-centered educational reform. These strategies were designed to strengthen and improve the academic performance and social behavior of students using principles and practices based in ancient and contemporary African culture, with a particular grounding in Nile Valley classical civilization (ancient Kemet/Egypt). African-centered educators in Oakland shared four fundamental beliefs.

> *First,* unlike many other ethnic groups in the United States, the legacy of slavery disrupted the cultural continuity and disconnected most enslaved Africans from an African identity and important cultural practices. As a result, African Americans in general—and students in particular—are disconnected from their African cultural roots that could provide practices, beliefs, life lessons, and worldviews fundamental for cultural survival and success in school.
>
> *Second,* the persistent failure that Black youth experience in schools is also due to the cultural incongruence of the curricula they encounter. Afrocentric educators therefore believe that students who come from different ethnic, racial, and linguistic backgrounds from their teachers will experience cultural incongruence in the classroom, which in turn can lead to academic failure.
>
> *Third,* African culture provides a pathway to cultural practices that hold the promise for self, social, and spiritual transformation. Many African-centered educators believe that through *Maat* (or *Ma'at*)—an ancient African (Kemetic/Egyptian) worldview based on truth, justice, propriety, harmony, reciprocity, balance, and right order—Black students, in the process of reconnecting with African culture, can become more empowered. Students who were fortunate enough to be exposed to these educators were encouraged with adages like "Think Maat, Speak Maat, Do Maat" as a foundation for skills and knowledge acquisition in the context of high moral behavior.
>
> *Fourth,* empowerment through African culture in service of identity development will translate to greater academic performance. This

is accomplished by teaching students about African and African American contributions and culture, using teaching techniques that are consistent with Ma'at, and creating curricula, across subjects, that are based on Afrocentric principals. Afrocentric education thus mitigates inconsistencies between the cultural backgrounds of teachers and Black students. During this second wave, Afrocentric education gained wide support as a promising strategy to remedy low academic performance in urban schools where Black students continued to perform poorly.

A number of key proponents of Afrocentric education in Oakland were instrumental in promoting the significance of identity and culture, and by extension supporting the academic achievement of Black students. Wave 2 efforts to support African American young people in Oakland were also supported by burgeoning research about the significance of culture and identity on the academic achievement of African American students. For example, *Countering the Conspiracy to Destroy Black Boys* by Jawanza Kunjufu, which was originally published in 1983, became a seminal book for many educators. It provided powerful analysis of the school failure of Black students, and specific strategies to remedy curricula and school policies in ways that promoted academic success. The ideas in the book offered educators an important analysis of why Black boys perform poorly in school, and practical strategies to reverse the trend of Black male failure. In Oakland, several rites-of-passage programs for African American young men deployed these strategies. For example, in the mid-1980s Dr. Wade Nobles created The Hawk Federation, his "manhood training" project for African American boys in Oakland. The Hawk Federation received national attention for being a model for working with young Black males. The Hawk project was informed by research conducted by Nobles and students at San Francisco State University, and it received wide support among Black educators throughout the country. Another significant contributor at that time was the Simba Program, founded in the mid-1980s by Roland and Elise Gilbert.

Wave #3: Institutional Responses, 1990–Present

By 1990, Oakland's efforts to address the academic outcomes of African American young men and boys had contributed to a broader dialogue among philanthropists and policy stakeholders about how to best support these youth. While local communities had been engaged with supporting African American boys and young men for years, several key foundations developed small portfolios focusing on Black males as a targeted population. Perhaps even more significant is how community residents, along with Oakland's Board of Education, boldly used research to inform policies aimed at addressing the academic achievement of Black students.

In the early 1990s, the Black United Front for Educational Reform (BUFFER)—a network of grassroots organizations and working-class activists that expanded to include professors, attorneys, and other professionals—set out to prove that OUSD was ill equipped to effectively educate Black students. Led by longtime educational advocate Oscar Wright, BUFFER occupied an important role in the civic debate about what it meant to educate Black children in Oakland. The organization was comprised of a cross section of Oakland's Black working-class community. Parents, community activists, church members, and clergy challenged both individual schools and the school district to provide a more equitable education for Oakland's Black students. The organization worked to gather documentation that demonstrated that OUSD, by design, tracked Black students into low-performance classes. BUFFER sponsored numerous community meetings, workshops, and conferences to raise awareness about the pervasive educational inequality in Oakland public schools. BUFFER's review of academic performance among African American students, and its examination of OUSD's budget, found that there was gross neglect on the part of the school district in providing the necessary materials, support, and equipment to McClymonds High School, a historically African American high school in Oakland. Their analysis of the persistent underperformance was based on the premise that public schools by design were set up to maintain a permanent Black underclass. In 1993, Oscar Wright filed a complaint with the U.S. Department of Education and its Office for Civil Rights alleging that African American students were being tracked into the lowest academic classes, and disciplined, suspended, and expelled at a rate greater than other races, for similar issues. The U.S. Department of Education and the Office for Civil Rights concluded that Mr. Wright's allegations were true and in 1998 issued a court decree to Oakland Unified School District to provide equal access to educational resources.

In 1995, the Oakland Board of Education formed a task force in order to investigate the academic performance of African American students in the district. The task force focused on the Standard English Proficiency program and determined that the district should prepare African American students in standard English proficiency. The task force provided an array of strategies that would be helpful in this goal. For nearly a year, the Task Force on the Education of African American Students worked closely with community leaders, parents, teachers, professors, and educational researchers in order to define and articulate a plan that would improve the language performance of African American students. On December 18, 1996, the task force presented its findings to the board of education.

The Task Force on the Education of African American Students argued that language competencies of African American students in Oakland were influenced by linguistic patterns from West African culture. The main argument the task force put forward was that "African American students speak and bring to school a 'primary home' language that is not standard English, and that their need for specially designed curricula; committed, sensitive, highly trained teachers . . . is real and must be addressed" (Task Force on the Education of African American Students, 1996, p. 2). The task force challenged the board of education to take bold measures to:

- Recognize African American Language/Ebonics as the primary language of many African American students.
- Add African American Language/Ebonics to all district documents, offering optional placement of students in classes or programs serving limited-English-proficient students.
- Provide access to all services, current or planned, for limited-English-proficient students to limited–English African American Language/Ebonics students (Task Force on the Education of African American Students, 1996).

The board decided in 1998 to adopt Ebonics as an official language (Bazely, 1996a, 1996d; Payton, 1996). Shortly after the board of education adopted the task force's recommendations, the media spun the story and sold it to the American public as another educational gimmick to garner more resources for Black students (Rodgers, 1997). The highly publicized story caught the attention of many educators, policymakers, and parents, who viewed the board's decision to make Ebonics an official language as a joke at best and irresponsible at worst. In a situation similar to the Afrocentric project at McClymonds, community members debated what they believed to be best for educating Oakland's African American students (Bazely, 1996b; Payton, 1996; Welcome to Ebonics II, 1996).

What is key about this debate is that it illustrates how race and class shape school improvement efforts for African American students in Oakland. For some Blacks in Oakland, Ebonics was viewed as yet another attempt by the district to remedy problems with ephemeral Band-Aid–like solutions. For others, the move signaled a bold and daring move to reclaim Black cultural and racial identity in the face of policies that often marginalized Black students (Bazely, 1996c; Brand, 1996).

A second feature of Wave 3 responses to African American student performance in Oakland was strategic philanthropic initiatives. During the 1990s, several foundations turned their research and policy attention toward expanding promising practices intended to promote the development of African American young men. National, regional, and local foundations were increasingly supporting initiatives focused on this population. These philanthropic efforts not only provided necessary financial support for new initiatives; they also catalyzed much-needed research about the status of this population.

For example, describing the dire need for movement around this issue, the Ford Foundation entitled its 2008 report, "Why We Can't Wait: A Case for Philanthropic Action: Opportunities for Improving Life Outcomes" (Littles, Bowers, & Gilmer, 2008). On a state level, The California Endowment and researchers from the Rand Corporation used a solutions-focused title for their paper, "Reparable Harm" (Davis, Kilburn, & Schultz, 2009). Together these reports laid the groundwork for philanthropy to focus on the needs of African American young men and boys. For example, *Why We Can't Wait* provided a detailed report of the trends in social science research related to Black males and highlighted the challenges inherent in conducting research. Furthermore, the report highlighted the gaps in practice and offered recommendations to policy stakeholders and public agencies.

Together, these three waves served as fertile soil in which to plant the seeds for what is now the African American Male Achievement Initiative in Oakland Unified School District. Oakland's rich history of activism, community engagement, and "unapologetically Black" culture served as a powerful catalyst and foundation to continue the work of Black educational excellence.

THE STORY OF AFRICAN AMERICAN MALE ACHIEVEMENT IN OAKLAND UNIFIED SCHOOL DISTRICT

The creation of the Office of African American Male Achievement was an expression of a long history of Oakland's educational activism. In 2010, community activists, parents, and religious leaders joined forces with teachers and with the support of the school board created the first school district in the United States with a dedicated office designed specifically to address the needs of African American male students. This extraordinary move was in response to years of dismal academic performance among the district's African American students.

Black male students in OUSD have high rates of chronic absence, and persistently perform lower on standardized tests than their counterparts. African American male students also face disproportionately harsh school discipline; in 2011–2012, African American males comprised 16% of the population, but accounted for 41% of the students who received one or more suspensions. Recognizing that past efforts to address the needs of Oakland's African American students had done little to improve these outcomes, Superintendent Tony Smith, together with Oakland's Board of Education and community partners, reviewed past efforts and concluded that African American students' educational needs were not being met. "Generation after generation, Black families were sending their children to school; but the ideals of an oasis of learning were met with the realities of institutionalized racism, low expectations, and marginalization" (Watson, 2014, p. 8).

The Office of African American Male Achievement's mission is to create the systems, structures, culture, and conditions that guarantee success for all African American male students in OUSD. By using data, AAMA identified entry points into schools, networks, and central offices to increase equity, improve cultural competency, and implement practices that support African American students. Using culturally relevant curriculum, innovative pedagogy, recruitment of African American teachers, leading professional learning communities, community engagement, and a host of other strategies, AAMA addressed the problem with a two-pronged approach, working at the systems level to transform adults, while directly serving African American male students to succeed in their current environment. AAMA advocates argued for "targeted universalism" to address the specific needs of African American male students. Building from john powell's research (2009), AAMA's targeted universalism argues that equity can be achieved by transforming the system to provide greater supports and opportunities to the lowest-performing group of students. Unlike strategies that are based on the premise that all groups require the same supports, protections, and opportunities, targeted universalism argues that targeted approaches provide a "proof of concept" that can then be implemented with others in order to advance progress toward positive outcomes for all people in an ecosystem. To make the point, consider the example of curb cuts in urban landscapes, which grew out of the need and desire of the disabled community to move independently. Now they are utilized by parents pushing strollers, travelers pulling roller bags, and shoppers with grocery carts. A targeted approach has become a universal, standardized feature that most of us take for granted (Blackwell, 2017). Therefore, if OUSD seeks to improve academic and social–emotional outcomes for all of its students, AAMA would help the district address African American male needs, which will, in turn, strengthen the district's movement toward cultural and resource changes that benefit all students.

Developing a Conspiracy of Care for Oakland's Students

Under the leadership of newly appointed Chris Chatmon, a longtime youth development innovator for Black young people in Oakland and former teacher and principal, AAMA began with a bold vision, and a woefully inadequate budget. Upon being appointed the executive director of AAMA by Superintendent Tony Smith, Chatmon initiated Phase 1, which included school site visits to listen to current realities of African American students, a citywide listening campaign of K–12 African American students, parents, teachers, and partners. He developed the rationale and data for the targeted focus on African American students to engage the community in what was framed as a "conspiracy of care" for Oakland's African American male students. Building from the term made popular in the 1990s based on Jawanza Kunjufu's book, *Countering the Conspiracy to Destroy Black Boys*, Chatmon offered a fresh twist. Rather than focusing on a conspiracy to destroy, he envisioned fostering a conspiracy of care—a compassionate and strategic plan of action to improve the outcomes for Black boys in Oakland. To accomplish this, Chatmon launched what he called an "outside and inside game." Outside, he would focus on identifying and building a dedicated cadre of community advocates who collectively shared a compassionate, strategic vision for supporting Black students in Oakland. Inside, he would focus on confronting policies, procedures, and practices within the system that contributed to poor academic outcomes.

Chatmon used two key ingredients to establish his "outside and inside game" for the office of African American Male Achievement. First, he used district data to highlight the disparities among African American male students. His goal was to present the community with data so that the community would see that "the house was on fire." He commented, "We found that 1 out of 3 African American male middle school students had been suspended, and 1 out of every 6 African American male high school students had been suspended." Chatmon's listening campaign involved all segments of Oakland, from the flatlands (working-class neighborhoods) to the hilltops (middle- to upper-class neighborhoods), and involved students, parents, teachers, and district officials. He learned early that for African American male students in OUSD, the school day was often unwelcoming, harsh, and simply irrelevant to their lives. "Why can't we have more Black male teachers, who we can relate to," students would say to Chatmon. These students' words made an indelible impact on Chatmon's thinking, and his strategy for AAMA's design. He also knew that creating this office was a rare window of opportunity. Superintendents in Oakland rotate like clockwork, and Tony Smith, a White, liberal, race-conscious leader, was willing to publicly use his White male privilege to call out these issues and support this project. But history shows that ardent visionary educational superintendents don't last long in Oakland. Smith was the Superintendent for OUSD for the first 2 years of AAMA and then left the district.

Community engagement was the second key ingredient in creating AAMA. Despite the superintendent's enthusiasm and support for the office, Chatmon simply had no budget, no staff, and no plan. Chatmon explained,

"Tony was a college linebacker and would use metaphors like, 'Run far and fast, and I'll get you the ball, Chris.'" For the most part, Smith provided Chatmon with a great deal of latitude to explore, innovate, implement, and develop the office; however, the office still was constrained with a very limited budget. To address this, Chatmon invited community members on Friday afternoons—a Technical Assistance Team—to meet with him to examine policies, review research, conduct site visits, and explore strategies that could be used in AAMA's work. By June 2011, Chatmon had formed a 25-member steering committee that would form the architecture and direction for AAMA.

AAMA's efforts to improve African American students' outcomes rejected the problem-driven strategies that had directed programming for youth of color in past efforts. Rather than focusing on prevention, for example, Chatmon and his team wanted to highlight the positive efforts of African American students. In June 2011, an African American student in Oakland scored 100 percent on California's standardized achievement test. When the child's mother approached the principal of the school to see if her son would receive recognition, she was dismayed to learn that the district didn't have a platform to celebrate these types of accomplishments. She approached Chatmon, and AAMA staff surprisingly found that 15 African American male students in OUSD had scored 100 percent on the achievement test. In response, AAMA created a celebration ceremony in recognition of the 15 students that made national headline news and provided AAMA with national attention. Chatmon's "conspiracy of care" had taken root.

In the spring of 2011, AAMA launched the pilot of the Manhood Development class, which was located in three Oakland high schools. The Manhood Development classes were designed to support African American male students' social–emotional needs, while helping to advance their academic skills. Chatmon had raised enough money to hire three part-time teacher/advocates to design the curriculum and work with young men in each of the schools. The program's curricular groundwork had been laid by its predecessor Dr. Wade Noble's Hawk Federation, but also introduced new material and concepts related to Black masculinity and self-mastery. Baayan Bakari, a teacher and seasoned advocate for Black young men in Oakland, created a curriculum focused on character development, history, and identity for Black young men called Khepera curriculum. The Manhood Development classes were led by African American young men who had a solid history and reputation in working with African American young men in the city.

When Tony Smith stepped down as superintendent in April 2013, AAMA became vulnerable to its many critics of the usefulness of the program. In fact, Gary Yee, the interim superintendent, had publically expressed weak support for the office. But two important events contributed to the growth and vitality of the program. First, when President Obama announced Executive Order 13621 on July 26, 2012, it was the first time a president had publicly acknowledged the education crisis for African American students. The order established a White House initiative that would, in collaboration with the Department of Education, develop policy aimed to repair and improve academic outcomes for African American students. The following year, the president announced the My Brother's Keeper Initiative, powered to galvanize public and private resources to support African American young men and all American young men of color. David Johns, the executive director of the White House Initiative of Educational Excellence for African Americans, contacted Chatmon to learn more about AAMA's work in Oakland. Within a couple of days, Johns and Chatmon were sharing notes and learning about each other's work. After Johns returned to the White House, he made several inquiries to OUSD about AAMA's budget, staffing, and funding structure. David Johns's advocacy prompted Gary Yee and other district officials to maneuver greater institutional support to the program. For example, Chatmon himself was not a school district employee, so the funding for his salary was administered by the Urban Strategies Council, a community partner, not an official district office, in the first year of the program, and then Partners in School Innovation (affiliated with the district) in the second and third year of AAMA.

Second, in 2013 the Urban Strategies Council released the State of African American Students in Oakland report, which publicly revealed that not much had changed for Black students since Oscar Wright's complaint in 1993. The report was made available to Russlyn Ali, assistant secretary for civil rights in the United States Office for Civil Rights, which triggered an investigation and a compliance review of Title VI. The office found that "African American students were disciplined more frequently and harshly than white students" and required the OUSD to rectify its discipline practices. The United States Office for Civil Rights conclusions provided even more community support and district support to ensure that the district was in compliance with its recommendations. These findings allowed the district to designate "race" specific funding in order to abate further federal intervention.

CONCLUSION

The African American Male Achievement program was made possible because of Oakland's rich terrain of activism and fertile soil for educational change for African American male students. Together educational activists, community residents, and parents carefully—and consistently—nurtured an environment where ultimately AAMA would take root. Three waves of efforts to support Black boys in Oakland, each offering its own nutrients, fostered a fertile landscape for AAMA to plant its roots, grow, and flourish. Today the program now serves more than 800 African American young men a day in 24 schools in Oakland, and is used as a model in five schools in San Francisco, three schools in Antioch (a suburb of Oakland and San Francisco), and six schools in Seattle. The Office of African American Male Achievement has carried the torch for justice forward for African American students in Oakland. While former superintendent Tony Smith created the opportunity for AAMA, it was the community that created the momentum to keep it going. Today the program continues to serve young men in the Manhood Development Program and creates culturally relevant curricula for teachers, innovative leadership and character development activities, family engagement opportunities, and college readiness.

NOTES

1. The Oakland Five was the name given to Percy Moore, the executive director of Oakland's federally funded antipoverty agency, and four others when the police used Mace to clear a meeting room and all five were arrested.

REFERENCES

Bazely, M. (1996a, December 22). Ebonics in perspective. *Oakland Tribune*, p. A1.

Bazely, M. (1996b, December 23). A retrospective on school board's Ebonics vote. *Oakland Tribune*, p. A13.

Bazely, M. (1996c, December 22). School board issues clarification. *Oakland Tribune*, p. A1.

Bazely, M. (1996d, February 22). Striking teachers' union modifies stance. *Oakland Tribune*, p. A1.

Blackwell, A. G. (2017, Winter). The curb-cut effect. *Stanford Social Innovation Review.* Retrieved from ssir.org/articles/entry/the_curb_cut_effect

Brand, W. (1996, December 28). Ebonics policy at crossroads. *Oakland Tribune*, p. A1

Brunson, R. K., & Miller, J. (2006). Young Black men and urban policing in the United States. *British Journal of Criminology, 46*(4), 613–640.

Bryant, R. (2013). *Empty seats: Addressing the problem of unfair school discipline for boys of color.* Washington, DC: CLASP

Bryant, R., & Phillips, R. (2013). *Improving supports for youth of color traumatized by violence.* Washington, DC: CLASP/Sierra Health Foundation.

Crouchett, L. P., Bunch, L., & Winnacker, M. (1989). *Visions toward tomorrow: The history of the East Bay Afro-American Community 1852–1977.* Oakland, CA: Northern California Center for Afro-American History and Life.

Davis, L. M., Kilburn, M. R., & Schultz, D. (2009). *Reparable harm: Assessing and addressing disparities faced by boys and men of color in California.* Santa Monica, CA: Rand Corporation.

Edley, C., Jr., & Ruiz de Velasco, J. (Eds.) (2010). *Changing places: How communities will improve the health of boys of color.* Berkeley, CA: University of California Press.

Ginwright, S. (2000). Identity for sale: The limits of racial reform in urban schools. *Urban Review, 32*(1), 87–104.

Ginwright, S. (2004). *Black in school: Afrocentric reform, urban youth, and the promise of hip-hop culture.* New York, NY: Teachers College Press.

Gitlin, T. (1969). On line at San Francisco State. In J. McEvoy & A. Miller (Eds.), *Black Power and student rebellion* (pp. 299–306). Belmont, CA: Wadsworth.

Hutchinson, E. O. (1994). *The assassination of the Black male image.* New York, NY: Simon & Schuster.

Johnson, W., Pate, D., & Givens, J. (2010). Big boys don't cry, Black boys don't feel: The intersection of shame and worry on community violence and the social construction of masculinity among urban African American males—The case of Derrion Albert. In C. Edley Jr. & J. Ruiz de Velasco (Eds.), *Changing places: How communities will improve the health of boys of color* (pp. 462–492). Berkeley, CA: University of California Press.

Littles, M., Bowers, R., & Gilmer, M. (2008). *Why we can't wait: A case for philanthropic action: Opportunities for improving the life outcomes of African American males.* New York, NY: Ford Foundation.

McEvoy, J., & Miller, A. (1969). San Francisco State "On strike, shut it down." In J. McEvoy & A. Miller (Eds.), *Black power and student rebellion* (pp. 12–30). Belmont, CA: Wadsworth.

Mincy, R. B. (Ed.). (2006). *Black males left behind.* Washington, DC: Urban Institute Press.

Noguera, P. (2009). *The trouble with Black boys: . . . And other reflections on race, equity, and the future of public education.* San Francisco, CA: Jossey-Bass.

Payton, B. (1996, December 21). Reaction to resolution is swift, but loud. *Oakland Tribune*, p. A1.

powell, j. a. (2009). Post-racialism or targeted universalism? *Denver University Law Review, 86*, 785–806.

Rickford, R. (2016). *We are an African people: Independent education, Black Power, and the radical imagination.* New York, NY: Oxford University Press.

Rodgers, T. J. (1997, March 2). Ebonics: Empty theories and empty promises. *The New York Times*, p. F14.

Sánchez-Jankowski, M. (1991). *Islands in the street: Gangs and American urban society.* Berkeley, CA: University of California Press.

Self, R. O. (2003). *American Babylon: Race and the struggle for postwar Oakland.* Princeton, NJ: Princeton University Press.

Spencer, J. P. (2012). *In the crossfire: Marcus Foster and the troubled history of school reform.* Philadelphia, PA: University of Pennsylvania Press.

Task Force on the Education of African American Students. (1996, December 18). *Policy statement* (Resolution No. 9697-0063). Oakland, CA: Oakland Unified School District, Office of the Board of Education.

Watson, V. (2014). *The Black sonrise: Oakland Unified School District's commitment to address and eliminate institutionalized racism, an evaluation report prepared for the Office of African American Male Achievement*. Oakland, CA: Oakland Unified School District.

Welcome to Ebonics II: The backlash. English spoken here, by African Americans. (1996). *Oakland Tribune*, p. A-1.

Wilson, W. J. (1996). *When work disappears*. New York, NY: Random House.

Young, A. (2003). *The minds of marginalized Black men: Making sense of mobility, opportunity and future life chances*. Princeton. NJ: Princeton University Press.

CHAPTER 3

Love Works

Manhood Development Classes and the Pedagogy of Black Male Instructors

Na'ilah Suad Nasir and Jarvis R. Givens

It was an ordinary day in the Manhood Development Program (MDP) class at Oakland Technical High School in the spring of 2011.[1] MDP classes were all-Black, all-male elective courses led by African American male instructors for 9th- and 10th-grade students, with some programs also at the middle school level. Brother Parker, the instructor, started a debrief session with students about their previous class discussion as they sat in their desks arranged in a circle. Unexpectedly, one student began drumming on the desk; and without notice a few others began to contribute their own additions to the now polyrhythmic beat that became background music as Brother Parker spoke. While fleeting, this moment could easily have been read as disruptive to the flow of conversation, perhaps disrespectful, and therefore a potential disciplinary moment. But Brother Parker responded in an unconventional fashion. He kept talking while walking around inside the circle of students; "Keep the drum going too," he said casually. Unfazed, Brother Parker elevated his voice a register or two above the drumming and continued with his class warm-up. The drumming soon stopped on its own, as the students grew weary. Later in this class session, the instructor asked these students to restart their impromptu drumming as he divided them into groups for an activity. He chanted over the beat they created, "ones over there, twos over there." At other times, he rapped over the rhythm to provide instructions or to reiterate some of the goals or themes that were discussed in the class. One might call this culturally relevant pedagogy; however, in taking the long view of MDP instructors' collective pedagogical practices, even these fleeting moments were about refusing conventional narratives about who these Black male students were and how they deserved to be treated.

Brother Parker's pedagogy illustrates how MDP instructors made pivots in real time to reimagine what some may have considered disciplinary moments for these Black male students. This was customary in the MDP classroom. To be clear, drumming (or rapping) was not an everyday occurrence, but there were many instances of MDP instructors taking moments that could be perceived as students challenging authority and instead adapting in a creative fashion to maintain student engagement and disrupt traditional configurations of power in the classroom. In fact, reframing what counted as a disciplinary moment was a key characteristic of the MDP classroom. Instructors responded to acts that *could* have been read as disciplinary moments in nonpunitive ways. These were intentional acts, conscious pedagogical decisions in these teachers' efforts to create spaces of empowerment for a group of students who all too often experience the harshest forms of discipline in school and in the world. As captured in the previous scenario, reconstituting discipline translated to recognizing students' cultural communicative styles as legitimate forms of expression, refusing to restrict the physical movement of students, and assuming student positive intent. Brother Parker chose to invite students' drumming on desks as a legitimate form of classroom participation, if channeled appropriately, and folded it into the flow of his lesson plan.

MDP instructors commented on how regimented Black male students typically are in schools, how closely scrutinized and restricted their bodies are. In order for the MDP classroom to be a site for supporting and nurturing Black boys these norms needed to be challenged. "They [are] regulated in terms of their energy," said Brother Parker in an interview. "Where can they express their natural energy? So I would purposely do things that you wouldn't naturally be able to do in other classrooms. Like 'Alright, class is getting rowdy. Let's have a screaming competition right now. Who can scream louder?' And it just gets out all of that energy, you know?" During class sessions, as students were working on assignments or having small group discussions, it was not atypical to see students walking around, sitting on top of desks working, or standing up at the windowsill writing in their notebooks. Brother Tonio, at Oakland High School, made a similar declaration about the need for his students to be able to shake loose from their typical regimented routine, where their ability to be children was severely restricted. "For them, for the young men," he worked to "create a safe space . . . in the middle of the school day, within the middle of their school house. . . . they can come in and just let their guard down, and learn, and crack jokes, and be little boys for a minute again."

Research captures Tonio's and Parker's admonitions that Black boys are denied their childhood and space to be boys in school. Ann Arnett Ferguson (2001) referred to this phenomenon as the "adultification" of Black boys, whereas scholars Michael Dumas and Stanley Nelson have recently argued that in the popular imagination and school practices, Black boyhood is rendered "unimagined and unimaginable" (Dumas & Nelson,

2016). Recent psychological research confirms how visual processing of Black boys by the general public often translates to these young men being perceived as up to 4 years older than their actual age; in addition, some research points to close associations of Black boys with apes and criminal stereotypes (Eberhardt, Goff, Purdie, & Davies, 2004; Goff, Jackson, Di Leone, Culotta, & DiTomasso, 2014). To negate this phenomenon in their classrooms, the MDP instructors worked to create a space where Black boyhood was possible and affirmed. Black male students were encouraged to let their guards down and be children—vulnerable, silly, and worthy of love and care.

"I really like having my house set up as being a place where I can just let my guard down, you know?," said Brother Parker. "So the classroom should be the same way. Otherwise, nothing else is gonna—nothing conducive to learning is going to happen, you know?" In imagining a climate for his class that was home-like, this MDP instructor was referencing more than just creating physical comfort for his Black male students. It was both political and pedagogical, this act of unapologetically imagining and naming his students as children, kids worthy of warmth, care, and compassion. A Black male student may be hailed as a "thug" on the street or as "disruptive" in his classroom, but he may also be hailed as "son" or "child" or someone's loved one when he enters his home. MDP instructors constructed empowering sites for Black male achievement within, yet against the broader educational system that Black males typically experience as sites of suffering and neglect. This was especially done through their pedagogical practices that reimagined discipline and the very idea of Black manhood with their students.

INSTRUCTORS VIEW DISCIPLINE AND NARROW UNDERSTANDINGS OF BLACK MANHOOD AS A PROBLEM

Fundamentally, the African American Male Achievement initiative and the Manhood Development Program were created to acknowledge and respond to the real challenges Black male students have in schools, precisely because they are Black *and* male. Black boys have an intersectional experience that is often represented by statistical indicators of underachievement; yet behind these numbers is a more complex story of how dominant narratives of Black masculinities have continued to shape how these boys are interpreted in school spaces and how their actions are read and experienced by others. The iconic narrative of Black males in schools has been consistent with their experience in the broader public sphere—they are disciplined and punished more frequently and with harsher sanctions than any of their peer groups (Ferguson, 2001; Noguera, 2009; Schott Foundation for Public Education, 2015; Skiba, Michael, & Nardo, 2002).

The leaders who designed the Manhood Development Program recognized the need to address both the issue of discipline and the presumed ideas about Black masculinities that instruct disciplinary practices. This was most apparent in the Manhood Development classes. Black male students' experiences with discipline in MDP classrooms both challenged and critiqued their broader experiences in school. This reimagining of discipline held a close relationship to the way instructors modeled new perspectives for students to understand their intersectional identities as Black male students in Oakland. These two tenets (reimagining discipline and modeling new ideas of Black manhood) were enacted pedagogically through the instructors of the MDP classes, as depicted in the scenario in the opening of this chapter.

The teachers of the MDP classes were not traditional teachers; most of their educational training came from community-based organizations; they were not credentialed and did not matriculate through traditional teacher training pathways. As Jerome Gourdine describes in Chapter 8, instructors were chosen not for their specific training background or credentials but for their approach to working with young people and capacity to teach Black male students from an orientation of community and love. Identifying instructors often resulted from community recommendations and publicizing the call for MDP instructors through community networks.

Consistent across all of the instructors' educational ideas was an explicit understanding that the work they were doing was counterhegemonic, a challenge to the normative ways in which Black males experience public schools and the world. For instance, after hearing about some challenging situations a few of his students were dealing with during a group check-in, Brother Perry declared, "I think what's important for us to understand, especially when we're all around each other and we're all struggling, is that one of the benefits of this class is that we can help each other and we can give advice for things when we can't get it in other places." All of the instructors expressed strong convictions to do work with Black boys with a sense of urgency. According to Brother Parker, the work he did with MDP was about "life or death. Where I feel, like, if we don't get 'em, the streets will get 'em, and it's death, whether it's in prison or six feet under, it's death, whether it's today or ten years from now, it's death." All the instructors described their moral orientation to the work they did as deeply personal, because they too experienced the challenges their students faced. Many of the instructors were from Oakland, and they wanted their classrooms to be spaces of healing and love, intentionally accommodating of Black boys' vulnerability as children in ways that do not often exist.

UNCONVENTIONAL STANDARDS OF DISCIPLINE AS A KEY
CHARACTERISTIC OF MDP PEDAGOGY

How we define the problem surrounding Black boys and achievement has a direct correlation to how we go about solving it. To this point, instructors were clear about two things: Black boys' experiences of discipline in schools were unjust, inhumane, and unloving; relatedly, Black boys' experiences with these harsh forms of discipline and low expectations was a riff on the dominant script of Black manhood as toxic and deserving of punishment. Students themselves expressed ideas about how other teachers perceive them outside of the MDP classroom.

> *Interviewer:* When you come in for the first time, what do you think your teacher thinks when she sees you?
> *Kenny:* That this boy finna be a troublemaker.
> *Interviewer:* You think before you ever start talking they think that you're gonna be a troublemaker? Why is that?
> *Kenny:* Just the way I show myself.

This student, like many others, went on to describe how his self-presentation made him vulnerable to being read in a particular kind of way— as "finna be a troublemaker." This student's embodied knowledge and understanding of how he was viewed in the eyes of others, his teachers in particular, connotes how a particular "racial storyline" functions as common sense about what Black male students are capable of and likely to do (Nasir, Snyder, & ross, 2012).[2] "Finna be a troublemaker" always means already in need of discipline. Black males are precluded from the presumed innocence extended to most of their peers—because of how they "show" themselves.

Black-male-student bodies enter public spaces and are shaped by a narrative that instigates anxiety. For instance, Janelle Dance recounts an incident where a group of high school students were taken for "gangbangers" by a White observer based on their dress. These racialized exchanges are a form of symbolic violence, Dance points out, that reflect the tendency to "look at Black and Brown males, not see them, and then, assault them with stereotypes and negative racial icons that exemplify the subtle and pervasive exercise of symbolic power wielded by the American mainstream" (Dance, 2002, p. 128). Scholars Gilberto Conchas and James Vigil relay young Black male students' sentiments about how media portrayals of Black men support various misconceptions of them as less capable and potentially dangerous (Conchas & Vigil, 2012). Even in their preteens, Black boys' intentions and actions are often "adultified" by school administrators, thus leading to harsher discipline than their peers (Ferguson, 2001).

Like Kenny, quoted above, Kayton believed that most teachers held controlling ideas about Black students that shaped disciplinary practices and expectations. Kayton shared, "The teachers—not all teachers, but some of these teachers—like, they expect us to like get kicked out of class and mess up and get referrals. But they don't expect the Asians to do that, so if the Asians do that, that's like a big surprise to them. They're shocked if that happens. But if for us, they—they see that everyday." What Kayton expressed here is that teachers understand it as normal for African Americans to "mess up" and thus think it is normal/natural to discipline them. In other words, Black students are more immediately presumed to be discipline-worthy subjects, subjects in need of discipline. As Kayton emphasized, this was not a onetime occurrence but a continual process that was reinforced by students' knowledge of how they're perceived by their teachers and the actualization of discriminatory disciplinary practices.

MDP instructors understood that their students were not the problem. Their students were children who, as a raced and gendered group, have historically been cast as hypermasculine, violent, and more than likely "finna be a trouble maker."

These instructors' classrooms became sites where students encountered discipline as corrective, yet caring and compassionate. Reflecting on how MDP instructors required students to do physical exercises to settle classroom offenses or to say positive affirmations about a classmate if one student offended another, the 9th-grader Malcolm stated, "He tries to better us. Like, the exercise helps us, not . . . tear us down." Reimagining discipline practices was fundamentally linked to reimagining manhood in these Black male instructors' classrooms.

When Tyrell was asked to share his thoughts about the way Brother Claude disciplines students in his class, he highlighted that the instructor talked with students on basic human terms and resisted relying on common punitive measures.

> *Interviewer:* Do you feel different about the way Brother C disciplines versus other teachers, or—
> *Tyrell:* Yeah, it's way different. 'Cause his is more of a talk, theirs is more of a "Oh, okay, we're putting this on your record." Basically, 'cause you know if you get a referral it's on your record now, and they like putting dirt on your record, but he [Brother C] not gon' do nothin'. He just gon' talk to you.

Tyrell understood Brother Claude's refusal to rely on typical disciplinary methods as a direct pedagogical move that was against the dominant racial ideology. Brother Claude instead used these moments to affirm students in more positive ways, signaling a stark shift in relations from what Black male students experienced in other learning spaces. The fact that Brother Claude was not "putting dirt on your record" signaled a different kind of care for this young student. Brother Claude saw him and his future as valuable, and he was conscious of not throwing dirt on this student's future as traditional discipline measures did for young Tyrell and his peer group.

MDP CLASSROOMS AS SITES TO REIMAGINE BLACK MALE IDENTITIES

> Sometimes as Black men we feel the need to kind of puff our chest up, when we, when we get out here, and you know, and, and present ourselves to be bigger than we seem before. . . . You know what I'm saying, so I want y'all to keep that in mind when, you know, sometimes, we all do it. I get it, last Thursday, I felt like I had to walk out here with my chest up. . . . I felt like I needed to, to be, strong, like hard. You know what I mean, because I was really hurting. I was hurting really bad on Thursday. Y'all seen it, I was, I was hurting. But I felt like I had to be like [he sticks his chest out to demonstrate]. And that just shows I teach y'all that you don't have to do that right? But even though I teach you guys that, it doesn't make me a hypocrite, it just makes me human. (April 26, 2012)

Brother Perry spoke these words to his students at Castlemont High School one morning while sitting on top of a desk in front of the classroom during second period. There were about 12 students in his class sitting at their desks arranged in a semicircle. This excerpt is taken from a longer conversation Brother Perry facilitated with his students about the concept of masculinity and how being "hard" had become a performative aspect of Black male posturing—a normative construction of Black male identity Brother Perry presented as unstable and worth challenging. He even presented himself as a vessel to model this process of deconstruction and reimagining.

While Black males were portrayed as hard and unemotional, anti-intellectual, and disconnected from the domestic sphere or family, in the context of these classes all of these dominant narratives were explicitly problematized. Furthermore, MDP instructors created opportunities for Black male students to talk through more complicated understandings of Blackness and maleness, while creating space for students to model nonstereotypical Black masculine identities. The process of trying on these new Black male identities was modeled through curriculum content, teacher-student relationships, and the relationship cultivated between students and their MDP classmates. The way MDP instructors cared for students and connected with them on basic human terms was mimicked laterally in the students' relationships with one another. Therefore, MDP classrooms became sites were students were offered resources for constructing healthy and positive Black male identities as children who could be vulnerable and who could care for one another. MDP instructors offered explicit ideas about manhood, found creative ways to model expansive ideas of Black manhood, and allowed students space to put these more expanded notions of Black manhood into practice—all of which functioned as "identity resources" (Nasir, 2011).[3]

DECONSTRUCTION AND INSTRUCTOR VULNERABILITY AS FIRST STEPS IN REIMAGINING BLACK MANHOOD

Let us return to Brother Perry and his ideas on Black masculinity. According to this instructor, Black men often felt forced to present themselves as cool, even as they felt hurt, anger, or perhaps anxiety. As opposed to acknowledging his hurt and frustration, he felt like he had to "puff [his] chest up . . . and present [himself] to be bigger." Brother Perry was critical of this practice, yet he confessed that he is also guilty of it at times. He went on to say that sometimes "We just wanna get home so we can just break down and cry. Which I did all night that night." In this moment, Brother Perry modeled that it is okay to be emotional and recognize one's feelings. This moment became an opportunity to name an alternative way of being that challenged the dominant representation of Black men as unemotional. In the process Brother Perry also challenged the shame Black men may feel about being hurt or wanting to cry (Johnson, Pate, & Givens, 2010).

Moving the conversation forward, Brother Perry referenced a quote from a film the class had previously watched. He noted: "there is a lineage of Black men who want to deny their own frailty." This MDP instructor wanted his students to understand how those who deny their emotions and the full scope of their feelings deny a core aspect of their humanity. Encounters like these in the MDP classroom demonstrate how the instructors' pedagogy incorporated strategic acts of role modeling. They weren't empty shells as Black male professionals—they too were complicated Black men. They presented themselves and their personal narratives as opportunities to extract lessons. In these moments they modeled vulnerability, presented conversations that expanded ideas of manhood, and simultaneously demonstrated radical acts of care for their young Black male students as child versions of themselves. Brother Perry leveraged his connection to his students as a "relational resource" to model and emphasize alternative approaches to dealing with emotions—approaches that do not perform or react to stereotypes but resist them. The repeated nature of these social-emotional conversations across class sites invited Black male identities in which the work of "dealing with your emotions" was presented as a critical part of Black manhood and an act of agency to reclaim one's humanity.

Brother Tonio expressed his intentional decision to be transparent about his lived experiences as a Black male with his students. He saw the idea of closing off his personal life from students to be counterintuitive to his mission in the classroom.

> So, it's to kind of really show them, this is what your life is going to be. . . . So that was my whole of just trying to create a classroom where it's safe, we're able to talk on like different things about life as being . . . especially becoming into a young man and being an African American male in society. So I just kind of just took, how I lived my life, you know, and just put it into the classroom.

As expressed by Tonio in the previous excerpt, MDP instructors occupied a unique standpoint as instructors to their Black male students, especially given the paucity of Black male teachers. Tonio was an "outsider within," as conceptualized by Patricia Hill Collins (1986). Collins grounds this concept in the experiences of Black women as domestic servants who were exposed to private spaces of Whiteness during the Jim Crow period. These women were perceived to be permanent fixtures in White homes (within), but they were always "outsiders" because they never fully belonged to White families. This marginal positionality became a site of knowledge production, whereby a particular analysis of race, class, and gender could be generated (Collins, 1986). In a similar manner, MDP instructors held an "outsider within" positionality within the overall school structure. The MDP instructors, as Black male community members as well as instructors, often positioned themselves as independent of the school structures they worked within; they were vocal about the particular challenges that Black male students experienced within schools and society more broadly. The instructors were aware of the currency their personal narratives as Black men from the local community carried; they intentionally leveraged this to connect with students personally and academically.

REIMAGINING BLACK MASCULINITY IN RELATIONSHIP TO OTHERS

Ideas about Black masculinity were constantly challenged in the MDP classroom, and much of the work of expanding the options of what Black masculinity could look like had to do with reimagining Black men's relationships to others. For example, there were numerous encounters that had to do with exploring the relationship between Black men and children. Another big theme was challenging conventional depictions of how Black

men are supposed to relate to women. Finally, a significant part of the
work in the MDP class had to do with constructing new ways of being
among themselves as Black boys. The centrality of this work was explicat-
ed to students by Brother Tonio head-on: "What we're gonna start diving
into is the concept of masculinity and what it means to be a man. And
that's one thing you guys are gonna have to learn on your own. But it's also
somethin' you can be given information about to learn how to conduct
yourself properly as you get to that point." These discussions offered opportunities to critique how these three types of relationships were typically
portrayed—including stereotypes of absent fathers, misogynistic conceptions of womanhood, and violent peer relationships. It is important to emphasize that the relationships constructed between the instructors and the
students were often used as a model to project what the terms of relations
between them as Black male students could look and feel like. The terms of
relations cultivated between MDP instructors and students helped to create
a setting that invited these young boys to inhabit their identities as Black
and male in new ways.

In one example, an instructor focuses on the students' future roles as
fathers: "When I have a son, I will teach him___." Brother Jay used this
sentence starter for his students' daily writing exercise and the young men
were prompted to privately write down lessons they wanted to pass on
to their male children. The crux of this activity centered around students
imagining themselves as caring and engaged fathers; it positioned them as
having the agency to foster this identity in the future. These dialogues became spaces where students discussed their relationships with their fathers,
and the instructors always participated. This particular activity supported
students in challenging societal stereotypes, and in some cases their lived
experiences, to reimagine new identity possibilities for themselves as future
Black fathers.

Demonstrating love for family and intimate interactions with their
children was another way that instructors employed their personal experiences to serve as a model. Brother Jonathon said in an interview, "Of
twenty-one of the boys [in his class], three grew up with their fathers so
I think it was important for them to have positive male images." The instructors, almost all of whom were fathers, frequently discussed their roles
as active parents in the lives of their children. For example, Brother Perry
reflected on how he enjoyed playing with his son every night before bed-
time. Likewise, Brother Tonio's daughter was a main character in many of
his stories—constantly highlighting that fatherhood and time spent with
his children was a valued aspect of who he was.

Instructors also pushed back against gender norms with respect to domestic tasks. Two examples highlight this: in one instance Brother Jay offered to cook something for a class potluck, and in another Brother Jelani

cradled a baby in his arms as he talked to his class. In both instances the students initially laughed, but Brother Jelani continued rocking the child and Brother Jay reassured the students that there was nothing wrong with a man cooking—that he actually does it often when he has friends and family over. In these moments, MDP instructors destabilized dominant notions of Black manhood and relaxed rigid boundaries about how Black men could engage the domestic sphere. At times students had immediate opportunities to try on these new constellations of Black male identity. For instance, Brother Jelani continued rocking the baby who came to the class with a visiting parent and he encouraged students to come "and make her [the baby] smile." These young men jokingly competed with one another to make the baby laugh and took turns holding her.

Similarly, in other lessons, instructors led explicit discussions about sexism and misogyny. In one instance, students were participating in an activity where they were asked to list items that give men status, and one student said, "girls." Taking this up as a teachable moment, the instructor stopped the student taking notes on the board. "I asked for items and women are not objects," he projected. The instructor declared that students must challenge their idea of women as "things." Through his comments, the MDP instructor modeled a mindset that encouraged a critique of the objectification of Black women and challenged dominant portrayals of Black men as misogynistic. The instructors intentionally offered new identity constellations of masculinity that were not dependent on the subjugation of Black women—in fact, it constructed Black masculinity as complementary with respect and humility toward others overall.

The care and love MDP instructors had for their students was acknowledged explicitly and regularly. These moments of emotional expression captured the terms of relation in the class—expressing love for others was a vital part of Black manhood. The teacher-student relationship in the MDP class was also an identity resource for how Black men should engage with one another. "This class is what I live for," said Brother Jelani. "You guys gonna get tired of me before I get tired of you." In this comment, the instructor explicitly acknowledged that the class and these boys had a place in his life outside of the classroom space. Furthermore, by noting that the boys would tire of him first, he let the students know that his care was unconditional. Another instructor commented, "I don't have to be here, I'm here because I care." Instructors found it important to verbally express their feelings for their students. One instructor commented on these verbalizations of care, "I think it was new for them in some ways. Because I had students say to me: You care. So you been with teachers you felt like didn't care? Yeah. No, no, Jelani cared. So it really made a difference."

Another instructor offered, "From a manhood perspective, you don't hear that enough between brothers . . . we need to show love to each other and to ourselves more often." Hence, the idea of instructors declaring their love for students was also about reframing the way Black males can and should interact with one another. Each instructor acknowledged their love for their students in a deliberate attempt to aid their students in reimagining themselves as loveable and as deserving of love.

While Black males are often stereotyped as "hard" or unemotional, these instructors supported students in reframing their understandings of who they were and reimagining who they should be with one another. Brother Jelani shared the following example from his class:

> There was one brother for example that was having a tough time.
> I said, "Uh, you know, he needs some extra love so lets give him
> a group hug." Of course he ran. And we all caught him. But
> afterwards, aaww, he was lit up. Like you could just see he was like
> [makes a huge smile], it just made his day. So, why do I go back to
> love? Because love works. If it's not rooted in my work then I'm just
> working, getting a paycheck. I don't do that. I'm beyond that.

Love in MDP had verbal and physical dimensions that challenged students' notions of acceptable manifestations of Black manhood and had a positive impact on students.

CONCLUSION

There is an insidious link between stereotypical ideas about Black manhood and how they influence lived social interactions of Black males with others in school. An accumulated body of beliefs and stereotypical images make up the dominant narrative about who Black males are, how they behave, and what they are capable of. These ideas about Black maleness and the threat Black masculinities pose to others and society has informed how they encounter disciplinary systems, in school and otherwise. Black males are presumed to be violent and in need of discipline; likewise, harsh discipline and punitive tactics disproportionately targeted at Black men continue to reify the idea that they are violent and in need of more discipline than others.

In this chapter, we have shown how MDP instructors put love at the center of their pedagogy to challenge both normative discipline practices experienced by Black males and the ideas about Black male students that informed said discipline. The first was by reimagining the role of discipline in classrooms by humanizing the actions and needs of Black male students, thus redefining the adversarial relationship between Black boys and schools (at least in the context of MDP classrooms). The second was by reframing the possibilities for Black male identity, and in doing so, pushing back against stereotypical notions of Black manhood that served to constrain and dehumanize the students.

The reconstruction of discipline was fundamentally tied to reimagining Black male identities in school. To see Black male students as worthy of compassion and in need of love and care over discipline meant seeing Black boys as children, as human. This was a critical step toward creating space for Black male students to be vulnerable with their peers and with the MDP instructor, whom they understood to be caring and nurturing. Reimagining discipline opened up space for more expansive ideas of Black manhood to be explored and modeled within the MDP classrooms.

NOTES

1. The content of this chapter is informed by 3 years of ethnographic research, including classroom observations and interviews with MDP instructors and students. The general themes discussed in this chapter extend from findings explored at length in the following works: Nasir et al, 2015 and Givens et al 2016

2. In this work, Nasir describes "racial storylines" as pervasive narratives of race and particular racial groups that people confront and contend with across social settings. These storylines are often the fodder—or taken-for-granted ideas—that shape ideas about who certain racial groups are "supposed to be."

3. In this work, Nasir argues that social and cultural spaces of learning provide resources that assist in the process of student development/identity formation. There are material, ideational, and relational resources present in learning spaces, as well as activities for students to take part in, which tell students things about who they are and who they can become. These resources become part and parcel of students' self-making process.

REFERENCES

Collins, P. H. (1986). Learning from the outsider within: The sociological significance of Black feminist thought. *Social Problems, 33*(6), S14–S32. doi:10.2307/800672

Conchas, G. Q., & Vigil, J. D. (2012). *Streetsmart schoolsmart: Urban poverty and the education of adolescent boys.* New York, NY: Teachers College Press.

Dance, L. J. (2002). *Tough fronts: The impact of street culture on schooling.* New York, NY: Routledge.

Dumas, M. J., & Nelson, J. (2016). (Re)Imagining Black boyhood: Toward a critical framework for educational research. *Harvard Educational Review, 86*(1), 538.

Eberhardt, J. L., Goff, P. A., Purdie, V. J., & Davies, P. G. (2004). Seeing Black: Race, crime, and visual processing. *Journal of Personality and Social Psychology, 87*(6), 876–893. doi:10.1037/0022-3514.87.6.876

Ferguson, A. A. (2001). *Bad boys: Public schools in the making of Black masculinity* (Reprint ed.) Ann Arbor, MI: University of Michigan Press.

Givens, J. R. (2016). Modeling manhood: Reimagining Black male identities in school. *Anthropology & Education Quarterly, 47*(2), 167–185.

Goff, P. A., Jackson, M. C., Di Leone, B. A. L., Culotta, C. M., & DiTomasso, N. A. (2014). The essence of innocence: Consequences of dehumanizing Black children. *Journal of Personality and Social Psychology, 106*(4), 526–545. doi:10.1037/a0035663

Johnson, W., Pate, D., & Givens, J. (2010). Big boys don't cry, Black boys don't feel: The intersection of shame and worry on community violence and the social construction of masculinity among urban African American males—The case of Derrion Albert. In C. Edley Jr. & J. Ruiz de Velasco (Eds.), *Changing places: How communities will improve the health of boys of color* (pp. 462–492). Berkeley, CA: University of California Press.

Nasir, N. S. (2011). *Racialized identities: Race and achievement among African American youth.* Stanford, CA: Stanford University Press.

Nasir, N. S., ross, k., McKinney de Royston, M., Givens, J., & Bryant, J. N. (2013). Dirt on my record: Rethinking disciplinary practices in an all-Black, all-male alternative class. *Harvard Educational Review, 83*(3), 489–512.

Nasir, N. S., Snyder, C. R., & Ross, K. M. (2012). Racial storylines and implications for learning. *Human Development 55*(5–6), 285–301. doi:10.1159/000345318

Noguera, P. (2009). *The trouble with Black boys: . . . And other reflections on race, equity, and the future of public education.* San Francisco, CA: Jossey-Bass.

Schott Foundation for Public Education. (2015). *Black lives matter: The Schott 50 state report on public education and Black males.* New York, NY: The Metropolitan Center for Research on Equity and the Transformation of Schools at New York University.

Skiba, R. J., Michael, R. S., & Nardo, A. C. (2002). The color of discipline: Sources of racial and gender disproportionality in school punishment. *The Urban Review 34*(4), 317–342. doi:10.1023/A:1021320817372

CHAPTER 4

The Khepera Curriculum and the Transformative Educator

A Dual Approach to Engaging, Encouraging, and Empowering African American Boys

Baayan Bakari

One of the reasons I believe I am on this earth is to support educating African American children to be deeply proud of who they are as a people and as individual persons. This curriculum and my work have been created in the spirit of all of those African American men and women who encouraged the enslaved, from the moment we as a people were brought to these shores, to never forget their humanity, dignity, and right to exist and prosper upon this earth.

I wanted to start with the above statement and perspective, because if you understand that, then you will ultimately be able to grasp the sincere intentions behind all of the content and pedagogical protocols that follow. Intentions matter. Education for African American children has never been about learning to read, write, and do arithmetic in any singular fashion. Education for our children has fundamentally been about freedom and healing. African American people were intentionally lied to about our heritage and, prior to emancipation, were threatened with death if caught reading, thus making it nearly impossible for us to find truth.

Given White supremacy's intentions to disempower African American people by miseducating us, we do not have the privilege to approach our students with the objectiveness many teachers and curricula endorse. Our students are assaulted culturally through music, television, marketing, websites, and social media—imagery that gives them the worst ideas of themselves. These assaults on African American students' identities also affect the mentality of non–African American people. The results of the Implicit Association Test, designed by Harvard faculty, have illuminated that all races, including African Americans, show a negative bias against African American people (Mooney, 2014).

I consider this negative perception within both African American students and the instructors who teach them to be the greatest threat to their educational success. I come to this conclusion not just from many years of personal anecdotal experience, but also from research. Ilan Dar-Nimrod and Steven J. Heine (2006) conducted research that shows that female math students who were told that male students were smarter genetically end up scoring lower than those who were not given this false information. This demonstrates the effect of belief in one's innate ability on achievement. Of course Claude Steele's (2011) work regarding stereotype threat makes the same point. The Pygmalion Effect research based on the work of social psychologist Robert Rosenthal and the recent work of Christine Rubie-Davies and her Teacher Expectation Project in Auckland, New Zealand, are revealing with respect to the impact of the belief of a teacher about the innate ability of a student. It was the subtle ways she spoke to the students she believed were smarter regardless of how they were actually performing that eventually led to their outperforming other students (Ellison, 2015). In short, expectations, bias, and self-efficacy are major factors in classroom success.

My curriculum and our pedagogical approach seek to nullify the impact of the cultural biases and low expectations of teachers in the classroom, while at the same time increasing the self-efficacy, esteem, and motivation of African American students. How we attempt to do this will be the focus for the remainder of this chapter.

The Khepera Curriculum gets its name from the Egyptian scarab, more commonly known as the dung beetle. The word *khepera/kpri* itself can be translated into "to become," "to change," or simply "to transform." The story of the dung beetle in Egyptian mythology is profound. Because the beetle places its eggs in excrement and then rolls the excrement ball across the ground, mimicking the path of the sun, it became symbolic for self-re-creation out of any situation with the help of the divine. To understand the need for the concept of self-re-creation by African American people, we can look at the life of Malcolm X. He re-created himself many times out of necessity and survival. His father was killed because of White supremacy and racial hatred at the hands of Americans of European descent. This tragedy resulted in Malcolm's choosing an identity of rebellion as he dealt with his pain. He also rebelled against an education system that taught him that he could succeed only by doing something with his hands, because the belief was that that was all "niggers" could do (X, 1987).

Malcolm left the school environment due to his righteous rebellion and was eventually arrested and sent to prison. Ironically, in prison he would learn history about African Americans that would inspire, encourage, and motivate him to re-create his identity again. This new identity was based on a refined understanding of himself. Reinvention is one of the most amazing aspects of Malcolm X's story. The need to self-re-create is such a profound reality in the African American community that President Barack Obama wrote in his autobiography that the most inspiring book he ever read was *The Autobiography of Malcolm X*, specifically because Malcolm had the audacity to forge his own cultural identity over and over again. As a people, African Americans are in great need of this ability. In this spirit, the Khepera Curriculum class taught within the Office of AAMA is called *Mastering Our Cultural Identity*.

The symbolic use of the khepera dung beetle and the class title were created with this historical understanding in mind. Without the ability of African American people to create our own cultural identity, we would be lost to destructive identities based on false history and narratives created by a people who desired us to be without dignity, grace, or intelligence.

There is one big thing to get out of the way before I go further into the concepts that are within the curriculum. This curriculum, and any other for that matter, is rarely effective unless it is paired with instructors and pedagogical practices that are in line with the Transformative Education model I designed for the Office of AAMA, which I detail in the next section.

THE TEN-POINT PEDAGOGICAL MINDSET OF TRANSFORMATIVE EDUCATORS

There are 10 specific approaches I teach facilitators of the curriculum to use when implementing it. However, before I delve into the 10 aspects I must first explain how I define a transformative educator.

A transformative educator understands that school for many students of color is as much about relationships as it is about instruction. When the Office of AAMA conducted its listening campaign, there was an over-whelming desire by African Americans to be seen, to be treated with the same kindness and respect as other students. They talked about needing adults in the school building they could relate to, people who would listen to them. These requests are all relational. Collectively, many people of color (justifiably) come to state and government systems with an apprehension and a certain level of skepticism; this *includes* the school system. Therefore, it is crucial that within the school walls African American boys feel safe and not threatened. Relationships with staff, instructors, and peers are crucial to feelings of safety and belonging. Bulletin boards, speeches, and sympathy won't do it; authentic concern for the well-being of the student is critical.

As a transformative educator, a teacher must genuinely care about the interests, hobbies, and activities of his or her students, right alongside their reading and math scores. The transformative educator doesn't "act" concerned but truly wants students to achieve *regardless* of how they may be conducting themselves at the moment. From this perspective, there are no favorite students.

In order to reach this level of understanding and authentic concern, a transformative educator has to tap into his own transformative journey and reflect upon what he needed and wanted at transitional periods in his own life. This is the most important of all for those who seek to work with students of color.

Transformative educators understand that whenever a student comes into the classroom and is not performing or is being consistently and inappropriately distracting, an *impact event* has occurred. An impact event is a moment that provides the opportunity to shape or reframe the relationship with the student. After the impact event is when instructors have their biggest opportunities to impact students of color who already have to contend with biased cultural, educational, and legal systems. This is when transformative educators lean in and address the issues or help the student find resources. They do not ignore students. This is anathema to a transformative educator. Every student matters.

Once it's clear that a potential facilitator possesses the character and temperament needed to be a transformative educator, we can then move on to instructing that facilitator in the basic philosophy and the pedagogical mindset that best serves this curriculum and approach. The following is by no means a detailed description of the concepts. Each one is essentially potentially a chapter itself, so I am attempting to give only a brief explanation of the ideas that constitute our training.

Brief Overview of Pedagogical Mindset

1. *Teacher roles.* Instructors are supported in understanding the multiple roles that they must be able to take up, including: being a teacher, where one's role is to present compelling information; being an educator, where one must draw out the excellence and optimal development of students; and being a facilitator, where one's job is to set up the environment for maximal engagement and learning.

2. *Multiple modalities.* Teachers are supported in learning to create a classroom environment that provides space for students to engage with multiple modalities, including sometimes sitting and listening, and other times engaging more actively. Teachers must ask themselves which modality the planned activities require of the students: Are they expected to be quiet? Can they move about

the class because this is a group activity? The need for a variety of modalities to be utilized during class is emphasized.

3. *Transformative educator.* Each facilitator must embrace the transformative educator characteristics, including recognizing impact events, believing that every student matters, and seeing care as an essential component of the classroom.

4. *Beyond Pygmalion.* Instructors must understand that it is critical that expectations remain at the highest level regardless of where the student starts. Failure is not allowed.

5. *Classroom leadership, not classroom management, is practiced.* The idea here is that students who have been negatively impacted by the educational system often have negative histories, which can result in a distrust of those in positions of authority. The teacher must be an authentic, fair, and capable leader.

6. *The curriculum + the relationship = success.* It is impossible to have maximum success with the curriculum if there is no relationship with the students in the class. The importance of building authentic caring relationships with students is emphasized.

7. *Collective genius.* The concept "collective genius" underscores the idea that we, as a community of instructors, hold genius collectively, rather than individually, and that we exist and work within a network of support. It also helps the facilitators understand the significance of leaning upon one another for support consistently.

8. *Culture & rigor.* Rigor must be maintained while our facilitators are teaching culturally and personally relevant content. That means that every lesson should be grounded in an academic concept or idea that the teacher believes is key to the lesson.

9. *Asset-based practice.* The facilitators must have an asset-based teaching practice. This means that students are viewed as community assets and are applauded and celebrated regularly.

10. *Teaching as a calling.* The facilitators must approach the work in the tradition of African American educators: This work is *a calling*, not just a career. In other words, teachers are encouraged to see their work as a life mission—as a contribution to humanity rather than simply as a job.

These essentials of the pedagogical mindset are the basis upon which effective use of the curriculum rests. Once teachers fully understand the pedagogical mindset, they are ready to begin to enact the curriculum.

THE KHEPERA CURRICULUM

The Khepera Curriculum consists of several courses, which can be used on their own or in conjunction with one another. The curriculum is dynamic and has been designed to evolve over time—a typical course provides not only written lessons, but also video links and additional sources, as well as accompanying readers in some cases. These courses are offered in the MDP program, and are also available to outside organizations and districts as a part of our consulting services. The following courses comprise the Khepera Curriculum.

1. African American Power in the U.S. (History Course, 10th Grade). This course is designed to explore how African Americans contributed to the intellectual, cultural, economic, and moral development of American society through resistance to enslavement and through the journey to power. The course follows African American history from the shores of West Africa and the kingdoms many left behind, through the Middle Passage, onward through the fight for emancipation and dignity, and up to the continuing battle for justice. The course offers critical insights into how cultural dynamics within a nation inadvertently contribute to the overall development of a young society. The course also analyzes how milestones or development of one cultural group can affect the trajectory and opportunity of other groups.

Often in U.S. History courses, African American history is limited to a chapter or two on slavery and then the civil rights movement. African American history is intellectually richer and offers much more to the understanding and analysis of how America has become the nation it is today. This history deserves at minimum a complete year during the American educational experience to explore the intersection between African Americans' struggle for power and the formation of the United States of America.

2. World's Great Men and Women of Color (History Course, 11th Grade). This course looks at world history through the lens of individuals. It is historically evident that certain people have come along and changed the course of humanity by the sheer force of their courage, compassion, intellect, ambition, or even desire for revenge. Students in this course understand how specific men and women of color, beginning in Ancient Egypt, have shaped the history and future of the world. Students understand and can articulate the correlation between ideas launched in antiquity and concepts societies stand on in the 21st century. Students are challenged to envision the world without these individuals and what might have been. By studying the biography of individuals, students learn the history, culture, and politics of the land that the historical figures came from.

The key assignments in this course emphasize more than historical dates and figures; they illustrate how those dates are actual signposts that mark historical progression. Students must synthesize the historical information they learn in relation to what they understand about current times. Analysis and critical thinking, in addition to creative, solution-oriented skills, are honed in key assignments.

3. Mastering Our Cultural Identity (Elective, 6th-9th Grades). Mastering Our Cultural Identity: African American Male Image sits at the intersection of contemporary youth culture and media, historical information, and the latest research in psychology and positive thinking. The course supports students as they explore the concept of cultural identity options and learn how successful individuals have managed their emotions and channeled their personal will to develop a positive sense of purpose in their roles in family and community.

Cultural identity is a key point of intervention for African American boys and young men, and Mastering Our Cultural Identity: African American Male Image focuses on creating opportunities that allow our students to make conscious, positive identity choices, thus better supporting academic trajectories, school engagement, and college and industry preparation for success during and after high school.

4. Revolutionary Literature (English Course, 10th Grade). Revolutionary Literature draws on contemporary and historical literary and nonliterary writings as students explore, analyze, discuss, and write about the internal struggle with cultural identity that African Americans face. Students specifically explore how African American men resist stereotypes in the United States and how to create their own identity, develop personal will, and build their future. Students also learn through selected narratives how African American men have managed their emotions and harnessed their personal will power to achieve their goals through reading, writing, and spoken word.

5. Arguments for Freedom (English Course, 11th Grade). This course explores the evolution of the cultural and political mindset of African Americans and White Americans from 1955 to 1975, during what has been called the civil rights era in American history. This course supports students in exploring one of the most impactful civil rights struggles in the history of the world through key literary texts that helped shape the perspective of participants of the movement. Students will also analyze in detail how the political perspective of the movement's participants shifted as the years progressed.

Upon completion of the course students will have gained a much more critical analysis of this tumultuous time in United States history than what is usually offered in standard textbooks. Students will have been exposed to writings and speeches of some of the greatest thinkers America has ever produced, such as Martin Luther King Jr., Sojourner Truth, and James Baldwin. Students will understand the cultural climate that led to the development of the civil rights era by reading newspaper articles, biographies, interviews, and portions of court documents. They will understand why the civil rights movement began and how it evolved into the Black Power movement, and will make connections to the Black Lives Matter movement that began after the murder of Trayvon Martin.

6. Classics Revisited (English Course, 12th Grade). This course explores the less common classics of Western literature that offer a more culturally diverse representation of the development of Western thought. Many people are aware of the contributions of Socrates, Plato, and Aristotle, but may be less cognizant of the Greek historian Herodotus, who is considered the father of history in Western literature. Within the course students explore the literary relationship between all of those characters and Egypt. Students read an interpretation proposed by George G. M. James's classic text *Stolen Legacy*, and must use comparative analysis to examine that book and the work of Herodotus and take a position on whether or not African innovation preceded Greek innovation.

7. The Depth of Hip-Hop (Visual & Performing Arts Course, 10th Grade). This course explores one of the most far-reaching and impactful artistic creations in American history: hip-hop. Hip-hop music is believed by many young people to be a monolithic art form focused on bravado and materialism. By taking this course, students will be exposed to the diverse genres and messages that are also available in hip-hop music and artistic expression. This course will focus on six albums and many singles that have had a profound impact on the development and consciousness of America's youth culture. Students will be exposed to the political, cultural, spiritual, and historic genres within hip-hop that were widely lauded and iconic. They will also be challenged with creating their own artistic expression using each of the genres they are studying, and will have the opportunity to understand all five elements of hip-hop culture: graffiti art, break-dancing, DJing, emceeing, and fashion.

Upon completion of the course, students will have expanded their knowledge of the origin and intent of the creation of a worldwide art form. They will have developed an appreciation of some of the most conscientious and positive content ever released by artists within the hip-hop community.

CONCLUSION

The courses and pedagogical approaches have all been uniquely designed to engage, encourage, and empower African American boys and young men while at the same time remaining rigorous. The curriculum and approach are dynamic and will continue to evolve as feedback and evidence illuminate different aspects of this work. Much like my life, this work is lifelong practice in healing and moving toward freedom of the mind for our young kings.

REFERENCES

Dar-Nimrod, I., & Heine, S. J. (2006). Exposure to scientific theories affects women's math performance. *Science, 314*(5798), 435.

Ellison, K. (2015, October 29). Being honest about the Pygmalion effect. *Discover magazine*. Retrieved from discovermagazine.com/2015/dec/14-great -expectations

Mooney, C. (2014, December 8). Across America, whites are biased and they don't even know it. *The Washington Post*. Retrieved from www .washingtonpost.com/news/wonk/wp/2014/12/08/across-america-whites -are-biased-and-they-dont-even-know-it/

Steele, C. (2011). *Whistling Vivaldi: How stereotypes affect us and what we can do*. New York, NY: Norton.

X, Malcolm. (1987). *The autobiography of Malcolm X* (As told to Alex Haley). New York, NY: Ballantine.

CHAPTER 5

What It Means to Do This Work

The Voices of Manhood Development Program (MDP) Instructors and "Politicized Care"

Maxine McKinney de Royston and Sepehr Vakil

Interviewer: Why do you keep on bringing up the word "love"?

Brother Jelani: Man, because young Black youth need it. They need it. They need to know that if I'm saying to you, "You know what, that's not a cool thing for you to do, to speak in that language, to talk to people that way," [then] that's loving. . . . When there's no love then there could be scrapping or even worse, but when there is love, there is an understanding that can come out of that. That's just my personal philosophy . . . I work with youth, that's based on love. Because I love myself and I love students. I love working. I love seeing that love come out of them. . . . I think from a manhood perspective you don't hear that enough between brothers . . . we need to show love to each other and to ourselves more often. And that's just simply believing in each other. You know, like, supporting each other. There was one brother for example that was having a tough time. I said, "Uh, you know, he needs some extra love so let's give him a group hug." Of course he ran. And we all caught him. But afterwards, aaawww, he was lit up. Like you could just see he was like . . . it just made his day. So, why do I go back to love? Because love works. If it's not rooted in my work, then I'm just working, getting a paycheck. I don't do that.

As Brother Jelani's comments demonstrate, MDP instructors saw their work as a labor of love. This labor involved intentionally creating strong and deeply caring teacher-student relationships. MDP instructors, like Brother Jelani, saw these relationships as necessary supports for Black male youth as they navigated their racialized and gendered realities. Unfortunately, these realities are part of the "hidden" curricula that constitute the schooling contexts students learn within (Apple, 2013; Ginwright, 2004; Thorne,

1993). MDP students themselves are keenly aware of how schools operate as racialized spaces and shared during interviews that they felt teachers held lower expectations of them (i.e., "just knew" they would fail) and that many of their teachers did not care about them or know them. Mirroring Brother Jelani's comment that without love he would just be "getting a paycheck," one 9th-grade MDP student said, " . . . like, the teachers, they just want the check; that's it. . . . Some teachers, they say they care, but I really don't think they care."

In this chapter, we argue that MDP instructors constructed relationships with students characterized by what we are naming *politicized caring*, an approach that encompassed centering the social needs of Black students and conceptualizing their roles as teachers beyond the confines of the classroom.

THE "WORK" OF MDP INSTRUCTORS: TEACHING AND CARING AS CULTURAL AND POLITICAL

For MDP instructors, being a teacher and mentor of Black male youth was more than a job, it was "life work." They believed that the social–emotional well-being of students should be a central focus and recognized it as a precondition for academic success. Brother Tonio, an MDP instructor at a high school, explained it this way: "Kids have a lot on their mind, probably have nobody to talk to at home or in the neighborhood. So, I think that, you know, it's [important] to hit on the curriculum piece of things, but we need to know what's on the kids' minds." Echoing these sentiments, Brother Jelani argues that Black male students struggle to be socially and psychologically healthy and successful in school because they lack the supports to do so. He believed that MDP helped students to "become better in class and it raises their character. But if their grades are slipping, it's all bad. Now if their grades are good and they're into some craziness, that's all bad, too. So, what we [MDP] gotta do is balance it."

This concern for students' social–emotional and academic well-being was reflected in the pedagogy of MDP instructors, and was also deeply connected to their understanding of their MDP students as Black male youth. During the instructor training hosted by AAMA, MDP's pedagogical approach was articulated as being based on high expectations, unconditional love and patience, and "Black male competency"—an understanding of the complexities of being a Black male in the United States. This articulation reflects a consciousness or "political clarity" about cultural and political dynamics that affect MDP students' lives as Black males, as students, and as Black children living in this country.

However, political clarity isn't solely in the heads of the MDP instructors; it guides their teaching and day-to-day interactions with their students. A key example of this occurred early in Brother Jelani's class. Trayvon Martin, an unarmed African American teen in Florida, had recently been shot and killed by a neighbor, who was not immediately apprehended by law enforcement. Knowing that this incident was on students' minds and might affect their disposition in school, Brother Jelani brought up the case and encouraged his middle school students to build stronger relationships with one another, and across the Black community:

> Realize that Trayvon Martin is . . . a human being . . . don't reduce his name to a slogan, . . . Pray for his family, his mother and father, and his family members. . . . The same problems also happen in Oakland, and sometimes it's not somebody outside our race. It's us against us. We have to love each other, respect each other, not immediately fly off of the handle with each other. Have more empathy towards each other; it's not really that serious. . . . We gotta be able to have that with each other. . . . And one extra thing: we gotta be closer.

Considering the students' psychological and emotional needs and seeking to create a space for their free expression, Brother Jelani asked us to stop recording. After the cameras and recorders were off, students shared their feelings and their own connections to feeling like they were Trayvon. Brother Jelani's culturally and politically guided instruction was not limited to that day, but was ongoing and particularly explicit in those days and weeks following Trayvon Martin's murder. He understood that while this tragedy occurred outside of school, it might also affect his students' experiences in school.

Shortly afterward, the school administration allowed students to wear hoodies to school in solidarity with Trayvon. That day, a student came into Brother Jelani's class and quickly sat down in a far corner of the class, away from everyone else. While other teachers might be irritated with this deviation from classroom norms, Brother Jelani realized that something was wrong. Calling out to him, he said, "J! Come on, man. You're in your safe space now, so come on out your hood. Pull your arms out. I know that you had a rough day, but you're amongst family so everything is cool now." The students shared that while most teachers were supportive, some teachers wouldn't let them wear their hoodies despite the administration's permission. Positioning himself as an advocate and as someone who cared for them, Brother Jelani questioned, "Did your hoodie stop you from studying? Did it stop you today?! Did it . . . impair your ability to listen and learn today?" Emphasizing their agency and capacity to succeed in spite of the circumstances, he went on to advise:

> If you really want to get justice for Trayvon Martin, there's one thing that you can immediately do: stay positive, stay on your focus, handle your business, don't allow these teachers to start trying to mess with you and jam you up the way they're trying to mess with Jaquan [another student in the class] right now . . . Don't let it happen; don't let it happen. Be smarter than that . . . You all know that you can make it through the rest of the year. You know these teachers; overcome that. That's the first thing that you can do.

In this way, Brother Jelani's interactions demonstrate how MDP instructors viewed their pedagogy as cultural and political work and often sought to develop students' critical consciousness and sense of themselves as capable of succeeding ("Be smarter than that"; "stay on your focus"). As in the example above, MDP instructors supported MDP students' own consciousness by supporting students' positive sense of self and their racial identities (see Chapter 3 of this volume), and by positioning themselves as adult allies to students who often experience hostility and opposition from school officials and other teachers.

FAMILY TIES: MDP INSTRUCTORS CREATED COMMUNITY WITH THEIR STUDENTS

The cultural and political consciousness and care integral to the pedagogy of MDP instructors was partly based on an embodied connection that MDP instructors felt between their lives and those of their students. One instructor expressed that MDP instructors needed to attend to this connection so that their students "wouldn't have to go through what I went through." MDP instructors saw their students as younger extensions of themselves and worked to be connected with the lives, families, and communities of their students. Instructors often called parents or had students call their parents during and outside of class, and held meetings with parents as a way to demonstrate that the development of their children was a communal responsibility that MDP instructors took up.

Brother Tonio taught an MDP class at a high school where he was already employed. Like Brother Jelani, he was seen by many students as a father figure, because "he's, you know, he cares about us and he's also on our backs sometimes, you know, making sure we get our work done" (MDP student interview). Brother Tonio viewed building community and incorporating family into his teacher-student relationships as a personal and professional responsibility that is "just what I do. You know, I found it easier going to the home, making home visits. I'm even dropping the kids off . . . that's just part of my job." Younger instructors like Brother Phil, an MDP instructor at another high school, made similar statements that revealed an orientation to his teaching as built upon a sense of community, personal connectedness, and care. True to his artistic roots as poet and performer, his teaching approach was very expressive and filled with thoughtful spontaneity, and he connected the violence his students experienced in their neighborhoods to larger histories of oppression facing Black people and Black men in particular.

Brother Phil shared that he was an MDP instructor because he wanted to lovingly counter the terror experienced by Black male youth and to give his students opportunities to be vulnerable and create a supportive community for and among themselves. "I think what's important for us to understand especially when we're all around each other and we're all struggling is that one of the benefits of this class is that we can help each other and we can give advice for things when we can't get it in other places." One way he did this was by being vulnerable about his own life and engaging in personal conversations with his students about their lives as Black male youth. During one class session, Brother Phil shared that his father had just died. Building on the close relationship with his students, Brother Phil talked with his students about the complicated feelings he had about the passing of someone whom he loved but who was also abusive to his mother. In doing so, he modeled ways for his students to be vulnerable and let their guard down, and to deal with their own feelings and emotional stress. This moment was clearly unplanned, and as such it reflects the truest sense of community—to open up and give oneself to the community. This interaction was emblematic of his caring orientation, his cultural and political consciousness about stereotypes surrounding Black men's emotions and hypermasculinity, and his constant efforts to build community with and among his MDP students (Givens, Nasir, ross, & McKinney de Royston, 2016). MDP students took note of the work that MDP instructors put into building community with them and often viewed them as father figures, or for some of the younger instructors, "more like a [big] brother than a teacher."

BLACK EXCELLENCE: MDP INSTRUCTORS
AFFIRMED THE HIGH POTENTIAL OF STUDENTS

MDP instructors' relationships with their students and their community-building efforts were also based on their cultural and political understanding that their students' willingness and ability to learn were intertwined with how the students were perceived and stereotyped. MDP instructors understood that Black male youth were frequently viewed through a deficit model, which included presumptions about their criminality, intelligence, and willingness to succeed. Brother Jay, another MDP instructor, explicitly linked his role as an MDP instructor with the need to address and disrupt academic and nonacademic stigmas of Black male youth. A lecturer in the African American studies department at a local community college and a credentialed teacher, Brother Jay's approach was deeply informed by how he felt Black male youth were stereotyped and treated:

> I think our boys, whether you want to believe it or not, are ostracized, marginalized. You know, they're seen as criminals. . . . I wonder what's the percentage of teachers that come in looking at our Black boys and say, "Wow, goodness" . . . and our boys feel it too. You ain't gotta say it. They see how people looking at them. . . . Because your perception already is that we criminals. . . . How you going to really get to know me? . . . That's what prejudice is. You have already prejudged who I am. . . . That's not knowing someone. . . . I think I'm working on changing that culture because that's what they do to us. That's what they do to black boys. And then we internalize it. We keep thinking we a problem. Then we don't want to come to class. Then we don't want to show up. We don't want to participate and they flunk you. Then they just fail you. That's what happens. And then they say, well, you wasn't participating. And it's because of him and his ability and him not, it's always the child. But you don't realize how you facilitated the child to check out.

Brother Jay articulates a consciousness—what we're calling a political clarity—about the stereotypes and racial microaggressions his students encounter in and out of school. He also articulates that Black male youth are likely aware of these stereotypes, and are in danger of internalizing and reacting to them. He connects his critique to the types of teacher-student interactions in schools that locate failure in the Black male "child" because teachers don't "know" them and "haven't built relationships with these kids." Brother Jay connects teachers' failure to get to know their Black male students, to have high expectations for them, and to build relationships with them as potential reasons for students' lack of respect for teachers or lack of willingness to participate. He argues that if teachers care for and get to know their students, they can set high expectations and students will meet those high standards. Like other MDP instructors, Brother Jay saw the need to affirm the potential of Black male students, including his MDP students, both as a pushback against racial and gender stereotypes, and as a way to support his students in living up to their limitless potential.

BLACK BOYS ARE CHILDREN: MDP INSTRUCTORS TREAT STUDENTS IN DEVELOPMENTALLY APPROPRIATE WAYS

In addition to holding high expectations and affirming the potential of students, MDP instructors stressed the importance of recognizing that they were working with adolescents. In his interview, Brother Tonio articulated that much of youth success in schools relies on teachers' abilities to understand their students as children with academic and nonacademic needs that are often interrelated:

> Just in general, kids want to talk. Kids have a lot on their mind, probably have nobody to talk to at home or in the neighborhood. So, I think that, you know, it's [important] to hit on the curriculum piece of things but we need to know what's on the kids' minds. Like, "What's your day looking like" . . . so a kid gonna tell you man like, "I'm not eating" or "I can't sleep" . . . then we can hit on that. . . . We need to take care of that before we can take care of anything else.

Above, Brother Tonio demonstrated how he views the holistic (social, physical, emotional, and academic) needs of students as individuals who are becoming adults, but who are still children with a diverse set of needs.

While Brother Tonio was thoughtful about how to address the diverse needs of his MDP students, in part because they were children, he was also thoughtful about his role as a Black male in their lives, given the distinct needs his students might have as Black male children:

> So, it [MDP] is to kind of really show them, this is what your life is going to be. You know, knock out your task and then you'll have time to kind of relax. So that was my whole [thing] of just trying to create a classroom where it's safe, we're able to talk on like different things about life as being—especially as becoming into a young man and being an African American male in society.

In the above excerpt, Brother Tonio recognizes that in MDP he is working with children who are on the crux of becoming adults and who may have been exposed to social stereotypes about what that means because of their race and gender. In recognizing this vulnerability, Brother Tonio sought to develop a safe, nurturing, developmentally appropriate classroom that could support students in navigating and resisting negative societal notions of Black manhood, a central component of politicized caring. Sharing a racialized gendered positionality with his students facilitated Brother Tonio's understanding of what his students may have needed to successfully enter adulthood. This intention also reflects the political clarity behind his work with his students; he saw his role as one of being a model for his Black male students, and he relied upon his own life experiences as an African American male to be vulnerable with and bond with them, and guide them through their own evolution and developmental trajectory.

MDP INSTRUCTORS' WORK AS "POLITICIZED CARE"

We've heard the voices of MDP instructors as they discuss how they conceive of their work and how they intentionally develop strong, caring relationships with their MDP students. We've seen the distinct quality of these relationships given the cultural and political consciousness and embodied knowledge that MDP instructors have about the in- and out-of-school lives and experiences of Black male youth. These forms of interpersonal care via relationships are, in part, an attempt by the MDP instructors to disrupt the dehumanizing schooling experiences of these youth (Walker, 1996). This ethic of care is part and parcel of the culturally relevant pedagogy that characterized Black schooling environments pre-desegregation and continues on in many all-Black classrooms and schools (Du Bois, 1935; Collins & Tamarkin, 1990; Fairclough, 2009; Foster, 1998; Lee, 1992; Walker, 1996). MDP instructors saw themselves, and were perceived by MDP students, as trusted mentors, protectors, and advocates.

Consistent with research literature, MDP instructors understood that teachers play a critical role in supporting students' academic and social development and experiences in schools (Dance, 2002; Eccles & Roeser, 2010; Libbey, 2004; Pianta, 1999; Roorda, Koomen, Spilt, & Oort, 2011). Positive teacher–student relationships are associated with improved student social functioning, engagement in learning, and positive academic identities and achievement. They also understood that the quality of teacher-student relationships was especially important for their students, who did not often benefit from positive teacher-student relationships because of racial and gender stereotypes (Noguera, 2003). MDP instructors saw their MDP students as a socially vulnerable population who were disproportionately disciplined and labeled with behavioral problems, and whose identities and actions were adultified, criminalized, and otherwise misconstrued (Ferguson, 2001; Gordon, Della Piana, & Keleher, 2000; Gregory, Skiba, & Noguera, 2010; Monroe, 2005). Finally, MDP instructors understood that teacher–student relationships are particularly critical during adolescence, when youth often seek out adult allies to support them in navigating multiple and at times contradictory social messages and contexts (Chhuon & Wallace, 2012).

The words of the MDP instructors demonstrate how they purposefully challenged deficit notions about Black male youth and color-blind notions of care. MDP instructors' form of caring was race-conscious and authentic to who they saw themselves to be and how they saw themselves in relation to their students (Noddings, 2013; Roberts, 2010; Valenzuela, 2010). We offer the idea of *politicized caring* to highlight the cultural and political intentionality that guided the MDP instructors' development and maintenance of their relationships with MDP students. Table 5.1 outlines the four themes of politicized caring that emerged from the voices of MDP instructors in this chapter. As the voices of the MDP instructors demonstrate, these themes are deeply intertwined and operate jointly to construct humanizing relationships between teachers and students that explicitly reject racial and gender stereotypes about Black male youth in order to offer counternarratives of resistance, personal agency, and self-worth. We argue that teachers' caring for their students becomes politicized—that is, a politics is enacted—when there is a connection between teachers' understanding of their students' lives and the translation of that understanding into the interactional life of their classroom. The politicized caring of the MDP instructors, for example, was conveyed through how they 1) talked about their "work" as involving being rooted in a political clarity and communal bonds, potential-affirming, and developmentally appropriate orientations; and 2) demonstrated these orientations through their pedagogical practices and interactions with their students in their classrooms.

This framework of politicized caring is an attempt to capture an approach that reflects the power and thoughtfulness of MDP instructors' voices and practices. Theirs is a method that nuances our understanding of how care is intentional, political, and remarkably visible. Their approach also highlights that the creation of a race-conscious, culturally relevant learning space relies upon an expansive conception by a teacher of what counts as their "work" and upon the enactment of that conception within the classroom practices of that teacher.

CONCLUDING THOUGHTS

In this chapter, we explored how MDP instructors thought about and intentionally created caring teacher-student relationships with their Black male students. MDP instructors saw these relationships as necessary to support these young people's navigation of the racialized terrain within and outside of schools. We also showed how these relationships were the fabric that created a positive learning environment for MDP students, one that challenged negative stereotypes and narratives about Black male students. Attention to the cultural and political aspects of care through relationships means that teachers attend to the "psychological, sociological, and academic needs" of their students (Walker, 1996, p. 131). At the crux of these teachers' pedagogy is a political bond with students that denounces

Table 5.1. Components and Descriptions of Politicized Caring

Description	Components
POLITICAL CLARITY (Beauboeuf-LaFontant)	
Clarity about institutional nature of oppression that shapes how Black educators understand and interact with Black students	• Understand students' connection to and experiences of oppression. • Cultivate students' awareness of racial and social injustices and discrimination or critical examination of American society (its history, institutions, and practices). • Understand students in context. For example, view violence in classrooms as microcosm of violence in Oakland and connected to systemic oppression; disciplinary practices in schools connected to stereotypes and treatment of Black males in U.S.
COMMUNAL BONDS (Morris)	
Community in the service of a racialized and politicized agenda, to disrupt systems of inequality	• Treat community as an extended family. View teacher-student relationship as more like surrogate family/fictive kin— "other mothers" or fathers. View students as extensions of themselves, understanding how students experience oppression. • Initiate relationships that recognize co-membership: building upon a shared racial, gender, class, or local background. • Establish a reciprocal relationship that views responsibility and success as mutual, and recognizes that the teacher's own future and success, and that of the community, are linked to that of their students.
POTENTIAL-AFFIRMING	
Affirming potential in order to disrupt a pervasive lack of institutional care	• Maintain high expectations. • Recognize that all students desire to learn and are capable of learning. • Build on cultural wealth, rather than assuming cultural deficits/poverty.
DEVELOPMENTALLY APPROPRIATE	
Developmentally appropriate spaces provided as a way to counter racist practices and views of Black youth	• Appreciate African American students as children situated along a developmental continuum that has a diverse set of domains and experiences: cognitive, emotional, social, cultural, etc. • Understand students' vulnerability as children living within racist social conditions.

Source: Beauboeuf-LaFontant (1999); Morris (1999).

the lack of care and racialized neglect within schools. Such race-conscious teachers embrace the often unspoken or invisible racialized and socializing aspects of schools and instead see their work as a "revolutionary antidote" (Ginwright, 2010).

The approach of the MDP instructors challenges how we think about Black male youth as vulnerable and pushes us to reconsider the work of teachers and what is possible within schools. The framework of *politicized caring* honors how certain Black teachers, and perhaps other teachers, acknowledge the ways schools reproduce inequalities and stereotypes, and work to cultivate relationships with students that recognize their oppression and their diverse needs as children. We offer the term *politicized caring* to emphasize how MDP instructors, within their own contexts, are (re)politicizing our notion of Black educators. MDP instructors remind us that ignoring or being blind to racialized and gendered stereotypes and the distinct cultural and social values in schools serves to continue the anti-Black status quo. These teachers are choosing to engage in the personal and political "work" of being an MDP instructor, in the "work" of developing strong, caring relationships with their students, to facilitate the personal and social emancipation of their students. MDP instructors purposefully place themselves, symbolically and physically, on the "front lines" in schools in support of their Black male students (King, 1991).

REFERENCES

Apple, M. W. (2013). *Education and power*. New York, NY: Routledge.

Beauboeuf-LaFontant, T. (1999). A movement against and beyond boundaries: Politically relevant teaching among African American teachers. *Teachers College Record, 100*(4), 702–723.

Chhuon, V., & Wallace, T. L. (2012). Creating connectedness through being known: Fulfilling the need to belong in U.S. high schools. *Youth & Society, 46*(3), 379–401.

Collins, M., & Tamarkin, C. (1990). *Marva Collins' way*. New York, NY: Putnam.

Dance, L. J. (2002). *Tough fronts: The impact of street culture on schooling*. New York, NY: Routledge.

Du Bois, W. E. B. (1935, July). Does the Negro need separate schools? *Journal of Negro Education, IV*, 328–335.

Eccles, J. S., & Roeser, R. W. (2010). An ecological view of schools and development. In J. L. Meece, & J. S. Eccles (Eds.), *Handbook of research on schools, schooling and human development* (pp. 6–21). New York, NY: Routledge.

Fairclough, A. (2009). *A class of their own: Black teachers in the segregated South*. Cambridge, MA: Harvard University Press.

Ferguson, A. A. (2001). *Bad boys: Public schools in the making of Black masculinity* (Reprint ed.). Ann Arbor, MI: University of Michigan Press.

Foster, M. (1998). *Black teachers on teaching*. New York, NY: The New Press.

Ginwright, S. A. (2004). *Black in school: Afrocentric reform, urban youth and the promise of hip-hop culture*. New York, NY: Teachers College Press.

Ginwright, S. A. (2010). *Black youth rising: Activism and radical healing in urban America*. New York, NY: Teachers College Press.

Givens, J. R., Nasir, N., ross, k., & McKinney de Royston, M. (2016). Modeling manhood: Reimagining Black male identities in school. *Anthropology & Education Quarterly, 47*(2), 167–185.

Gordon, R., Della Piana, L., & Keleher, T. (2000). *Facing the consequences: An examination of racial discrimination in U. S. public schools* (Research report). Oakland, CA: Applied Research Center.

Gregory, A., Skiba, R. J., & Noguera, P. A. (2010). The achievement gap and the discipline gap: Two sides of the same coin? *Educational Researcher 39*(1), 59–68.

King, J. E. (1991). Dysconscious racism: Ideology, identity, and the miseducation of teachers. *The Journal of Negro Education, 60*(2), 133–146.

Lee, C. D. (1992). Profile of an independent Black institution: African-centered education at work. *The Journal of Negro Education 61*(2), 160–177.

Libbey, H. P. (2004). Measuring student relationships to school: Attachment, bonding, connectedness, and engagement. *Journal of School Health 74*(7), 274–283.

Monroe, C. R. (2005). Why are "bad boys" always Black?: Causes of disproportionality in school discipline and recommendations for change. *The Clearing House: A Journal of Educational Strategies, Issues and Ideas, 79*(1), 45–50.

Morris, J. E. (1999). A pillar of strength: An African American school's communal bonds with families and community since *Brown. Urban Education, 33*(5), 584–605.

Noddings, N. (2013). *Caring: A relational approach to ethics and moral education*. Berkeley, CA: University of California Press.

Noguera, P. A. (2003). The trouble with Black boys: The role and influence of environmental and cultural factors in the academic performance of African American males. *Urban Education, 38*(4), 431–459.

Pianta, R. C. (1999). *Enhancing relationships between children and teachers*. Washington, DC: American Psychological Association.

Roberts, M. A. (2010). Toward a theory of culturally relevant critical teacher care: African American teachers' definitions and perceptions of care for African American students. *Journal of Moral Education, 39*(4), 449–467.

Roorda, D. L., Koomen, H. M. Y., Spilt, J. L., & Oort. F. J. (2011). The influence of affective teacher–student relationships on students' school engagement and achievement: A meta-analytic approach. *Review of Educational Research, 81*(4), 493–529.

Thorne, B. (1993). *Gender play: Girls and boys in school*. New Brunswick, NJ: Rutgers University Press.

Valenzuela, A. (2010). *Subtractive schooling: U.S.–Mexican youth and the politics of caring*. Albany, NY: SUNY Press.

Walker, V. S. (1996). *Their highest potential: An African American school community in the segregated South*. Chapel Hill, NC: University of North Carolina Press.

CHAPTER 6

My AAMA Journey

Teaching and Leading in Service of Young Kings

Jahi

My AAMA journey begins in San Francisco at the jazz club Yoshi's, performing with KRS-One. I'd returned to the Bay Area after spending the last year and a half in my hometown, Cleveland, Ohio, doing some work with a local nonprofit around hip-hop and the arts. When I arrived back to Oakland I heard about the new African American Male Achievement initiative just as I had begun making some life decisions. One was to really make Oakland home as long as I was going to live in the United States. Two was that I wanted to spend more time working with youth and education, as my musical career had taken up most of my time over the past decade—traveling, performing and writing music—so a sense of community was something I wanted to build.

This brings me back to KRS-One and Yoshi's. KRS-One has been a mentor, brother, and friend since 1998. Whenever we are in the same city and we have a concert we always reach out to each other and ROCK it. Out of all my heroes, KRS-One is the biggest reminder of who I am and the skill I aim to represent in hip-hop culture. We had a good night rocking San Francisco as always. Yoshi's San Francisco has since closed down, but thankfully it was open and live on this night. After the concert, a comrade I know from the music scene in San Francisco introduced me to Chris Chatmon.

Chris enjoyed the concert, had good vibes, and when he slid me his card I lit up. This was the brother I had heard such good things about with the African American Male Initiative. We agreed to connect right away, so a few days later we were having a formal sit-down in his office at the Paul Dunbar building on 2nd Street in Oakland. What impressed me most about Chris right away was he was a father with sons, and he actively cared for them and his family. Having sons myself, it means a lot to me to meet fathers who are involved and engaged.

I mentioned to Chris that I was living in the Glenview district and wanted to get involved with a school in my neighborhood. I was surprised to find out that Chris's sons attended Edna Brewer, the middle school right down the street. This conversation led to me joining AAMA, and pioneering middle school programming for the initiative. My work would take place in after-school settings. We didn't have an official curriculum at that time, but what we did have was vast and rich curricula from our previous youth work experience and management, which created a brain trust of new ideas. Edna Brewer was my first school, and in October 2011, I joined the AAMA team.

STARTING OUT IN THE WORK: EDNA BREWER

I was at Edna Brewer Middle School for two years. My top five accomplishments over those two years would have to be increasing attendance of African American boys in 6–8th grades, our Yoshi's Oakland performance, bringing KRS-One to Edna Brewer, our attempt with African American family engagements, and building with these young kings.

Reflection on a King—Eric

"Alright, Jahi, I'm about to roll." This is what Eric said to me as he was about to head off to college. He had some obstacles in getting everything together, meaning financial aid and paperwork, but he did, and was on his way to the airport. When I gave him a hug and a pound, I remembered that this was Eric, the 6th-grader in my first MDP class, about to head off to college. In terms of building our own pipeline, meaning ensuring that students were school-, college-, and community-ready, Eric was the first young man I saw go through the process for 6 years and, with AAMA's help, get into college. It was a big moment. Eric transformed from a young king with no college aspirations and battling with obesity to a scholar who played football and baseball.

Moving On

After a tumultuous year at Edna Brewer facing racism head-on, I decided to move to another school. The principal was clear that he did not want me back. After our last encounter when we discussed how to handle the defaming of a Black History Month bulletin board, it was clear we would never see eye to eye and really were unable to work together. The principal was unwilling to protect the bulletin board, and I worried that this reflected a lack of understanding and commitment to Black students.

TRANSITIONING TO CLAREMONT

My next stop was Claremont Middle School. It was a relief to be there, because there were two African American male principals, brothers, Reginald and Ronald—a blessing. They spent the serious time needed to set a school climate and culture with positive energy, affirmations, and high standards. Our style of working toward positive youth development was in sync. I taught the last two after-school MDP classes before we transitioned into an elective course during the school day.

Reflection on a King—Kevin

Kevin was a young king at Claremont who was a handful, to say the least. Spirited, funny, athletic, smart, and rugged, he was in the 6th grade. He was adopted by a young man named Charles because Kevin's parents were unable to care for him. We were working on attendance and attitude, and during these support sessions I found out that he liked to play chess. Kevin had many successes as a middle school student, but also some very traumatic and disappointing events. Charles, his adoptive brother, is now working with AAMA as a facilitator and is excelling in his work. Kevin is now in foster care with another family. I never could have imagined this would be the reality. I often think about Kevin, hoping that the life lessons he received from people at school and in the community who truly cared about him take root, that he'll continue to get help and do the right thing on his journey.

My second year at Claremont proved to be one of the most revealing periods of my life. I realized I was maxed out on teaching. I think all too often there are a certain number of teachers who reach this point, know it, and yet continue to teach. This, for some, leads to burnout. I've seen it in my years of being involved in schools. I didn't want to do that, and I wanted to get involved in leadership in AAMA. Chris has always looked out for me, but this was the first time we were not able to align in a next step for me, and it really came down to capacity, and I understood that.

I took a job as a director of a Boys and Girls Club in Menlo Park for about 6 months as I transitioned out of AAMA. I gained some valuable experience, including managing a budget of one million dollars and a staff of 7. But I also realized that working with AAMA provides an authentically Black space and way of being that you don't see as much in more corporate structures. The corporate world is diverse, but not equal. There were no Black folks in leadership in this new space, and I had a big problem with this. At AAMA I always knew that Chris and I had genuine respect for each other, and if I returned I could still be about the business of making a difference in the lives of youth.

RETURNING TO AAMA

Chris and I had breakfast one summer afternoon and discussed my returning. We were open, honest, and in the spirit of the movement and brotherhood I returned as a program manager for the Manhood Development Program. Personally, I felt a sense of pride because it created a new lane: a facilitator who could actually advance into management. As I write this and now see the possibility of multiple facilitators currently teaching who are interested in management, and are being considered for promotions, for me this was a legacy point.

Managing MDP is freeing. It's life changing. It's what I thought of as a meaningful route to help in my community. It's the balance to my musician side. It's what I was told you do as a musician, an artist, and a preserver of the higher principles of hip-hop: Serve your community. When I was in the classroom I had the ability to help transform a class, their parents, and a school. With MDP, as a program manager I could support and transform communities with the AAMA team, serve African American young boys and men who truly deserved it, and share my knowledge and expertise with the facilitators I would manage. It's the moment, as they say, when passion and purpose meet.

I have learned many lessons in my work with AAMA over the years. Here I share my top five lessons:

1. You cannot move in isolation. Working with AAMA is the only time in my working career where I truly know I'm a part of a team where I can stand in my truth and give and receive respect from everyone in brotherhood and sisterhood, and be about the serious work of making it happen and making a difference.
2. Social–emotional learning is vital. I never heard this term until I had a chance to build with Matin Abdel-Qawi, the principal at Oakland High School. The idea of valuing the social and emotional state of a king while working on academic excellence is something I practice today.
3. Working from assets is powerful. I'm not the creator of the idea that a young person should be loved, valued, respected, and appreciated—that he or she should be seen as important, with a voice, and possessing innate greatness, off top. But when I had to do a report once, I had to synthesize what I thought AAMA's approach was; it's asset based, not punitive or negative. That's

our difference. There are times where young kings will engage in actions that are detrimental to themselves, but even in conflict we attempt to come at our youth from a solution-oriented framework, allowing them to grow in the process. We come from a perspective that young people are assets to our communities, to our world, and to our families and our people. This is critical in working with African American boys, who too often see more of a negative depiction of themselves in the media than a positive one.

4. You've got to pace yourself. When your passion and purpose align, time can stop, meaning it's not about working 9 to 5, but about living your life's purpose. The lines can be blurred between work-and-life balance. This is a lifestyle, but work cannot be your life. I've learned that this work is more of a marathon than a sprint; this realization has helped me to operate on my highest level in my ability to help others. As the old folks in my family used to say, "You are finding your stride." I'm able to focus and go deep in helping facilitators and AAMA overall, and take good care of myself because I have learned to pace myself.

5. Students need to see you being Black and being proud. Young African American boys respond well when they see grown men show up and really care and be present. It's a great live-in-the-flesh example of how to be your authentic self and do something good in the community. We live in a place that is home to the Black Panthers. This is not a coincidence. It really helps in our image and approach to represent Black excellence in our own way and in our programming. We are not the answer, but we are a solution to the problem of underrepresentation and support for Black boys. Unapologetically.

CHAPTER 7

It Makes Me *Feel* Like I'm A Monster

Navigating Notions of Black Damage in This Work

Patrick Johnson and David Philoxene

I think it was the *San Francisco Chronicle* that came in and taped us when we had this discussion about "where we are yesterday, where we are today, and where we'll be tomorrow," and everybody was saying good things that are like . . . deep and that you could understand . . . but they perceived it as Black male students are at risk. Most of the pictures [they took] were of us in school having fun, laughing—one was of a student reading . . . *So I don't understand how they could say that we were at risk at all.*

—Manhood Development Program participant

In the above excerpt, the MDP participant demonstrates an awareness of the prevailing narratives of Black damage associated with young Black males as well as an understanding of how media advance such discourse. For this participant, a chasm exists between representations of the Manhood Development class observed by local media and his experience in the program. Despite seeing evidence to the contrary, the *San Francisco Chronicle* reporter is read as demonstrating an investment in linking young Black males to abjection and nihilism (Tucker, 2012). A *Newsweek* article about Oakland's MDP classes relies on similar conceptualizations of Black males (Nazaryan, 2015). In vivid narrative form, the article suggests that the work of MDP aims to "whisk the city's young out of Oakland, to Silicon Valley, to San Francisco, to any place that is better than this place they have always known." The article then lists a series of statistics said to capture "the plight of Oakland's young Black boys," suggesting to readers that "Black men are the nation's outcasts, marked like Oedipus for doom from birth. They are more likely to ditch school, more likely to be arrested, more likely to end up in prison. When they are not forgotten, they are feared. When they are not scorned, they are pitied."

This chapter raises concerns about the ways that MDP operates within the context of narratives about Black males as inherently damaged and considers how MDP participants may internalize such rhetoric, despite MDP's intentions to provide counternarratives. While the chapter concurs with other scholarship that underscores how the "Black Male Crisis" rhetoric informs current intervention policies targeting Black boys as "exceptionally" damaged, our primary goal is to explore how Black male students take up and potentially internalize the ethos that often undergirds such reform efforts. We are concerned with understanding how young Black males feel and experience the narrative of "Black damage" and how such narratives impact Black boys as they construct their racialized and gendered identities. We also highlight MDP's role in combating such narratives.

This chapter is guided by the following questions: How do MDP participants interpret the program's emphasis on Black male achievement? How must programs like MDP contend with the rhetoric that is often espoused to justify targeted intervention efforts? What do these narratives offer Black male students about who they are and who they can become? We recognize that rejecting the milieu of public discourse about Black males is one of the inherent challenges in doing targeted interventions. We argue that paying attention to the voices of young Black males who participate in targeted interventions such as MDP not only deepens our insights about how Black maleness is framed popularly and politically, but also equips educators and other youth development practitioners with the ability to anticipate the ways that Black males are impacted by the very narratives that targeted interventions seek to address. We hope that this chapter serves as a caution for those running targeted-intervention programs who, like MDP practitioners, are critical of flat depictions of Black male students' experiences. Participants credited their positive interactions with MDP instructors and their experiences with the program with helping them combat the deficit-oriented ideas espoused about young Black males in broader society.

We found that students' understandings about the need for MDP fell into three different categories, which we have labeled "We're the problem," "We need to be fixed," and "Against all odds." First, we look at how the idea of the inherently damaged Black male informs public policy discourse and social science research.

REPRODUCING BLACK DAMAGE

While it is beyond the scope of this chapter to engage in a rich discursive analysis of related policy language of Black-male–targeted interventions, such verbiage helps to contextualize the broader damage-centric nature of societal discourse about Black males and the context of programs focusing on Black male achievement. Such reform language and programs help to shape how young Black males understand their identities and remain the implicit rationale behind the emergence of targeted-reform efforts. These processes further entrench narratives about Black maleness and situate how student participants understand these programs' objectives.

In his remarks announcing the launch of the My Brother's Keeper initiative, President Obama positioned himself within a narrative of Black damage. Obama told a story about participating in a meeting at a manhood development program in Chicago. The president told the young men that when he was younger he "got high without always thinking about the harm that it could do" and that he did not always take school seriously. He told the young men that he "made excuses." Obama reduced his racialized and gendered experiences as a Black male to poor decisions, and in doing so leveraged prevailing sentiments about Black males to sell My Brother's Keeper to the American public. In this sense, Obama frames Black males as being complicit in the narrative of Black damage. Paul Butler (2013) argues that the idea that Black men are worse off than any other group continues to purport the allegory of Black men as an "endangered species," a narrative that often reinforces stereotypes about Black manhood and reproduces patriarchal values. The language Obama deploys has long proven effective in galvanizing attention to the issue of Black males.

Crenshaw (2014) observes, "Fixing men of color—particularly young Black men—hits a political sweet spot among populations that both love and fear them." Dumas (2016) finds the MBK initiative to be "an exemplar of neoliberal governmentality, in which Black young men and boys are constructed as essentially damaged, as a problem in need of a technocratic public-private solution" (p. 94) . While MBK may give rise to beneficial programs, as some other neoliberal initiatives have done, it undermines "more fundamental change by locating the problems within (the bodies of) Black boys and young men of color rather than in the social and economic order" (Dumas, 2016, p. 97). Much of the policy language around MBK framed the opportunity gap through efforts to highlight the lack of Black male opportunity and the limited nature of structural and institutional resources.

Despite these important (and often explicit) policy intentions to articulate external social impediments rather than intrinsic deficiencies of Black maleness, such enumerations (like the statistics detailed in the print articles and in Obama's address) run the risk of signifying to Black males that the cards are stacked against them. Dumas and Nelson (2016) note there is a dire need for research that explores how "Black males construct their identities at the intersections of race, class, and gender and within the structural and cultural forces of school," including these targeted interventions (p. 43). One way to do this is by prioritizing the voices and perspectives of Black males within the dialogue (Howard, 2008). With this in mind, we turn to the voices of MDP students to understand how the narratives of Black damage that are so pervasive in targeted intervention efforts affect how young Black males understand their racial and gendered identities.

MDP STUDENT PERSPECTIVES

Student interviews revealed that the young men sometimes understood Black male intervention programs as working to address the perceived deficiencies of African American boys.[1] As a result, these young men indicated both that they needed to be fixed *and* that the broader society created the conditions for them to actively fail. These themes did not emerge in isolation, but usually emerged in their conversations with one another. In the process, it became apparent that some students built on the common societal narrative and conceptualized the MDP class as an intervention to *fix them* and solve the problem that *they* represented.

We're the Problem

All of the students interviewed understood the MDP program to have a symbiotic relationship to the perceived deficits and failures of Black males as a group. In essence, they were the problem and the program was the solution. Students articulated this Black male "problem narrative" in multiple ways. They shared their awareness of how Black males were "trying to drop out" of school, "going to jail," or "in the streets." Furthermore, students shared their awareness of how these racial storylines of the Black male—as a problem, and as damaged—were mapped onto them by others.

In sharing his thoughts as to why the MDP class was created, Myles stated that it was "because most of our Black, African American males are trying to drop out of school and some of them just don't have the confidence to go back and they're like 'nah I can't do that man.'" Here, Myles articulated a narrative of Black male students as insecure in their scholastic abilities and, as a result, "trying to drop out." For Myles the problem of his particular race-gender group exists primarily at the level of individual choice and disposition. He goes on to say, "Me personally, I'm interested in improving while I'm in school and with this class I've been getting better grades." In the second half of his statement, Myles underscores that the problems, or damage, common to most Black males was not necessarily the case for him, although his resolution is still one about (albeit better) personal decisionmaking. This was a common theme in the interviews, where many students identified "the problems" with

Black male students as the motivation for the MDP class, yet simultaneously distanced themselves from the damage narrative. Thus, *students articulated their awareness of Black male damage as the central motivator
for targeted reform efforts, yet resisted accepting this narrative as deter-
minate of their own identities.* Essentially, these young men were saying,
"*These classes were created for Black males because they are damaged;
however, while I am Black and male, I am not one of them. I'm not like
the others.*"

In discussing the creation of the MDP class, Jarrod suggested, "They
probably created it because like, most African American males don't do
nothing with they lives and then they want to like help us, I guess . . . Yeah
like, they drop out like, some African American males drop out of school."
Here Jarrod offers a lack of self-determination or drive as a motivator for
the MDP classes. He suggests that "most" African American males lack the
ability to do something meaningful with their lives, and MDP can act as an
intervention to assist them in being more productive. Jarrod conceptualizes
the MDP class as working to supply students with greater ambition and as
a means of encouraging them to "want to do [something] with their lives."
Similarly to Myles, Jarrod positions this as "most" Black males, therefore
leaving space within the discourse for him to be positioned outside of the
damage narrative. However, even if these students did not see themselves
as similar to the majority of Black males who need the MDP class, it was
still a narrative they had to contend with in their own identity formation.
Even as they constructed their own identities, they intentionally positioned
themselves against a deficit, racialized storyline about Black males. Despite
MDP's best attempts, the power of the narrative looms large, shaping how
students make sense of the program.

In this same vein, students also believed that Black males were read by
others through a deficit lens. They articulated that even when silent, they
were viewed by others as a problem, as "probably going to drop out."

Many of the students observed that they were constantly treated as
always and already damaged, even when they were in new spaces. As Nick
stated, "They have different expectations of the Black male" than of other
groups of young people.

In describing how this recurring understanding of his identity impacted
his daily life, Raymond stated, "It's just outside, when I'm walking down
the street and outside the school and like somebody else walking and they
see I'm Black and they'll walk or they push they kids on the other side of
them and it makes me *feel* like I'm a monster or something." Raymond's
words suggest that confrontations with the perceptions of Black male damage are consistent occurrences in his daily life. The racial storylines that
inform these interactions and identity confrontations are sustained and reproduced by the national rhetoric of the Black male crisis.[2]

Needing to Be Fixed

While the students in this study articulated that the narrative of damage overdetermined how they were viewed in society, they also demonstrated a comprehension of MDP as an effort to help or fix them in addressing their problems. Student responses evinced that much of the rhetoric employed by those trying to help Black males in society reifies them as problems, while constructing Black males as things needing repair. However, it is important to reiterate that MDP worked to dissuade such thinking. Students consistently described what they identified as overwhelmingly positive experiences in the program. They were effusive in their praise for how their instructors empowered them to critique the distorted storylines advanced about young Black males outside of MDP's walls. However, the power of the Black male damage narrative is reinforced in multiple spheres in students' lives.

When Damien was asked, "Why do you think the school created this class that you have with Brother Jelani?," he shared that it was an effort to help Black boys lead more positive and productive lives:

> *Damien:* To basically get Black brothers like me to get out of the community and stop the getting in trouble, going to jail, stuff like that, and getting shot. To basically keep 'em up in they academics and stuff. Ya know . . . Just keep 'em off the streets.
>
> *Interviewer:* Hmph, what gives you that impression? What makes you think that's why the class was created?
>
> *Damien:* Because most of the people that I know are either shot or in jail.

Here we see Damien echoing the national rhetoric around Black male interventions. He articulates a notion that Black boys are constantly "getting in trouble," "going to jail," "getting shot," and always "on the streets." Given these dire circumstances, he understood the work of MDP to be aimed at addressing challenges occurring at the individual level. Therefore, students understood the classes as opportunities to help them make better choices. Students also expressed an awareness of the structural impediments to making such choices. While students are aware of the language used to justify programs like MDP, this is incongruent with both students' experiences in the program and how they describe their experiences.

Students identified a number of approaches being used to help them overcome their challenges—things such as learning about their history, group conversations about the challenges they face as Black men, and learning to "control their emotions." After being asked about how the lessons in their class related to their experiences as Black males, Nick stated,

"We're learning about self-control." Thus, the students saw emotional management and resocialization as a strategy of their MDP class, which directly implicates the prevailing narrative of Black males as being behaviorally challenging. The students presented the case that programs such as MDP helped them recognize alternative possibilities and see how behavioral adjustments could potentially fix their problems. Lawrence, for example, talked about how being more intentional about one's self-presentation could be a potential strategy. In referencing the killing of Trayvon Martin, Lawrence suggests that

> first impression of people with hoodies on is like ohh they gonna do something bad so that's why Trayvon Martin was being watched. You carry yourself well like button ups and just, not . . . don't wear hoodies in general.

Therefore, the students implied that there were ways of fixing themselves and behaving that could alleviate how the world responded to them, the problem. Maybe if they could adjust their attitudes or fashion themselves differently, their life chances could be positively impacted.

In offering his understanding of why the class was specifically for Black male freshman students, Marquise offered the following:

> To start them off early in high school so they can actually like go to college and stuff like that . . . like as a freshman . . . and then like, so like they won't get em later on in high school when they already messin up.

Therefore, he saw the MDP's targeting of Black male freshmen as fixing young Black males "early in high school," thus suggesting that as young Black boys get older they become more prone to messing up. Marquise suggests that the MDP class wanted to intervene in the lives of Black boys early on, before they progress to the stage of "already messin up,"—which, according to dominant narratives about Black males, is an otherwise inevitable fate.

"Against All Odds"

Just as the students understand the rationale for why they are targeted by intervention efforts, as Black males they also feel that individuals, institutions, and structures unfairly target them, limiting their social mobility and in some cases their very ability to live. Much of the intervention discourse implores Black males to change their personal behaviors, without addressing the pervasiveness of ideology and practices that construct

Black males as problems. In the dominant narratives chiding Black males for their perceived deficiencies, critiques of the asymmetrical power relations that inform their everyday lived experiences are muted. As counters to the prevailing frames about Black males, some students offered social critiques that highlighted institutions' culpability in perpetuating the idea that Black males are exceptionally damaged. As explored in preceding chapters, MDP instructors regularly addressed these ideas during their classes. Robert commented that the course was developed so students can "understand more about the world, the economy, and how it's against Black kids nowadays." Therefore, even if they did not find these critiques in the narratives of Black male reform efforts, based on their lived experiences and knowledge gained on the ground from family, coaches, and their MDP teachers, students articulated their views of how racism impacts their lives.

Several students stated that the adults in their lives, in talking to them about being Black males, stress that they are held to a different standard than their non-Black peers. Roderick commented that his football and basketball coaches "always say it's harder to be a Black man than anything else because we all have odds against us." Ishmael echoed these sentiments, suggesting that, "It's like when you Black you got like three strikes already, or two strikes against you already."

Students described Black males' relationship with the criminal justice system as particularly adversarial. Roderick's belief that law enforcement unfairly targets Black males is informed in part by learning about the prison-industrial complex while participating in MDP. He notes that African Americans are often frequently incarcerated for minor offenses. Damien argues that the idea that Black males are predators influences how police interact with them:

> They always think that because you're Black, you're troublemakers. That's not all true, too. I mean you see Mexicans being troublemakers and they don't really do nothing about it. White people? They don't really do nothing about it. With Blacks, they already at your door. Kicking it down just to rush you.

Students were particularly sensitive to what they saw as the devaluing of Black males' lives by the criminal justice system. This is best summed up by Marcus's thoughts on Trayvon Martin's and Oscar Grant's murders:

> If a Black cop killed a White person, like it'll be way different. A Black person wouldn't get off . . . His house probably get[s] shot up or something. Or he'll get the death penalty. It'll be all type of stuff. I just think that's racist but I can't do nothing about it. I just let it go.

Students exhibited agency in identifying the forms of oppressions that affect how they navigate the world. Both Damien and Marcus explicitly name how racism manifests through the criminal justice system, and thus impacts Black males' interactions with that institution. However, in addressing problems with Black males, intervention discourse relies on the familiar tropes of framing Black males as *the* problem. As a result, intervention efforts are stagnated by their inability to fully understand that issues with Black men are reflective of the larger structural and ideological issues related to White supremacy and patriarchy (Curry, 2017).

These young men articulated critiques of the ways racial ideology continues to function through structures that target them; thus, we see a contrast in how they articulate the problem juxtaposed with the metanarrative of "The Black Male Crisis." While these young men surely internalized the storyline of the socially deviant Black male in their conceptualization of the problem, they also pointed to the structural forces that largely go unnamed in the national rhetoric. The sense of hopelessness that many of these students expressed regarding "the problem" was facilitated by the gap in their attentiveness to structural oppression. Structural oppression is not mentioned in the so-called reform efforts that the nation hurls *at them* rather than *at itself*. Therefore, while Marcus explicitly offers his belief that the system he's up against is racist, the nation's resistance to seeing his reality pushes him to "just let it go."

CONCLUDING THOUGHTS

Relying on the voices of student participants in the Manhood Development Program implemented in the Oakland Unified School District, we have highlighted the ways in which Black boys internalize the pervasive narratives of the Black male problem. Through this discussion, we admonish policy and programs that frame Black males as "the problem." Doing so only continues to relegate the root of social inequity to poor choices of individuals instead of the structures of power that function to dominate. This framing centers on false notions of meritocracy, which allow for oppression to go unnamed. Although MDP instructors and leadership worked to counter Black male damage rhetoric, we recognize there is a need for greater vigilance in offering students the language to fend off these ideas. One way to accomplish this is for MDP to explicitly address how it diverges from the language that guides broader intervention effects, while remaining steadfast in its critiques of the practices—including the very policy language that helps bring programs like MDP to fruition—that locate the problem in Black males themselves.

Kiese Laymon (2014) argues that the rationale undergirding intervention efforts like MBK is shortsighted and fails to address the larger structural and ideological issues that plague all Black children. He writes:

> If the president isn't willing to even say the words "Black love" or "White supremacy" or "patriarchy," he can be a Black boy's keeper, but he can't be an honest lover of Black boys. They're trying to fix Black boys on the cheap, without reckoning with White supremacy. You fix a "what." You don't fix a "whom." What really needs fixing?

The policy language of targeted reform efforts operates from meritocratic beliefs that suggest if Black males just work hard, behave more respectably, and stay encouraged, their futures will be brighter. While this may work for some, it can in no way address the widespread oppression faced by people of color in urban communities. MDP students and instructors demonstrated an awareness of the flaws of such logic and articulated critiques that put their personal experiences in conversation with structural issues. However, despite the MDP's best intentions, the ubiquity of Black male damage rhetoric throughout broader society made it difficult for students to divorce such ideas from their understanding of the program. For this reason, it is crucial that targeted reforms make concerted efforts to examine the ideological and structural barriers to positive youth development for young Black males.

MDP worked to help students move beyond a focus on individual choices to explicitly name structural forces that sustain oppression in marginalized communities. As other chapters in this volume explore, this must be done at the level of policy and especially on the ground among those who work with Black male students on an interpersonal level as teachers, mentors, and advocates (see Camangian, 2010; Howard, 2008). We call on such leaders to be more intentional in arming Black boys with strategic identity resources that allow them to imagine more expansive possibilities for their future. This requires countering the narratives of Black damage that are readily available for Black boys.

This notion of Black damage has been offered up for social consumption and to young Black boys as an explanation for the challenges they face. The recurring narratives of Black damage continue to assault the humanity of Black people by naming them as the problem while concealing how racism continues to explicitly and implicitly structure our daily lives. Black boys are forced to think that they are the problem, and exceptionally so, given that little, if any, attention is given to the similar challenges faced by their peer groups—namely Black girls. The narrative of Black damage continues to function as taken-for-granted common sense for Black boys. Furthermore, this narrative muffles and distorts Black achievement and excellence, which is rarely recognized as part of the contemporary landscape.

Damage-centric narratives of Black manhood are pervasive in popular discourse, and thus an endemic ideational resource that Black male students have to engage with in their identity-forming process. It is a racial storyline that they are confronted with on a continual basis. Even if they choose to distance themselves from the narrative of Black male damage—as several students articulated—they must contend with it nonetheless. It is always present, functioning in the racial discourse that pervades the imagination of the American public. It becomes the lens through which African American boys are forced to interpret the meanings of Black and male at the point where they cross—the very intersection at which they are expected to find and locate themselves.

While this chapter is explicitly about MDP, we believe that students' experiences in the program and the ways MDP offers counternarratives to dominant understandings of young Black males offer insights for similar programs across the country. Our goal is not to prescribe what targeted interventions should look like, but rather to raise attention to the fact that conversations about Black males are often one-sided and paint a picture of Black males in perpetual crisis and exceptionally deficient. Moreover, we call attention to how we talk with young Black males about their societal "reality." There is a need for nuanced, compassionate conversations that are mindful about allowing Black males to collectively think, conceive, and dream outside of dominant narratives of Black male damage. This requires looking at young Black males as "social thinkers" with "the capacity to interpret the world around them" and "actively compare their situations to those of others" (Young, 2004, p. 11). Recognizing young Black males' ability to act as social thinkers challenges flattened narratives that construct them as "menaces who are inclined toward violence, or as a downtrodden and dispirited constituency that lashes out at the world with brutality and insensitivity" (Young, 2004, p. 11). While we actively resist haphazardly laying damage-centered discourses on the laps of young Black males, we acknowledge the very real challenges associated with being Black and male in the United States. However, it is through cultivating young Black males' ability to read the world and their place in it that we recognize their ingenuity, resilience, and humanity.

NOTES

1. Our data corpus consists of video footage and interviews collected in a study of the Manhood Development Program (MDP) implemented through OUSD's Afri-

can American Male Initiative (AAMA). The AAMA task force was created in 2010 to address the educational challenges faced by Black male students in the district (17.3% of OUSD's students). The data in this study were taken from a total of seven school sites over the span of 2 years, September 2010 to June 2012. A total of 54 interviews were conducted, including 48 from students and six from instructors. Additionally, a total of 37 class observations took place across sites. During these classroom observations the researchers set up a stationary video camera in the corner of the classroom, and sat in the back of the class while taking field notes. The researcher did not engage in class activities unless he was explicitly asked to do so by the course instructor. The footage and field notes captured various classroom interactions, instructors' pedagogical choices, and discourse with students. While this chapter is informed by all the data collected in this process, we draw particularly on the student interviews. These interviews were semistructured and took place during the last month of the 2011–2012 school year.

2. Nasir (2012) describes racial storylines as those persistent societal narratives about race that people have to account for and contend with, across a multitude of social settings, including schools.

REFERENCES

Butler, P. (2013). Black male exceptionalism?: The problems and potential of black-male-focused interventions. *DuBois Review*, *10*, 485–511.

Camangian, P. (2010). Starting with self: Teaching autoethnography to foster critically caring literacies. *Research in the Teaching of English*, *45*(2), 179–204.

Crenshaw, K. W. (2014, July 29). The girls Obama forgot. *The New York Times*. Retrieved from www.nytimes.com/2014/07/30/opinion/Kimberl-Williams-Crenshaw-My-Brothers-Keeper-Ignores-Young-Black-Women.html

Curry, T. (2017). *The man-not: Race, class, genre, and the dilemmas of Black manhood*. Philadelphia, PA: Temple University Press.

Dumas, M. (2016). My brother as "problem": Neoliberal governmentality and interventions for Black young men and boys. *Educational Policy*, *30*(1), 94–113.

Dumas, M., & Nelson, J. (2016). (Re)imagining Black boyhood: Toward a critical framework for educational research. *Harvard Educational Review*, *86*(1), 537–557.

Howard, T. (2008). Who really cares? The disenfranchisement of African American males in preK–12 schools: A critical race theory perspective. *Teachers College Record*, *110*(5), 954–985.

Laymon, K. (2014, March 17). Hey mama: A Black mother and her son talk about language and love in the South. *Guernica*. Retrieved from www.guernicamag.com/features/hey-mama/

Nasir, N. (2012). *Racialized identities: Race and achievement among African American youth*. Stanford, CA: Stanford University Press.

Nazaryan, A. (2015, March 25). Fighting to reclaim the future of Oakland's young Black men. *Newsweek*. Retrieved from www.newsweek.com/2015/04/03/oak-town-mans-316548.html

Tucker, J. (2012, May 23). Oakland schools' black male students at risk. SFGATE. Retrieved from www.sfgate.com/news/article/Oakland-schools-black-male -students-at-risk-3577141.php#photo-2328722

Young, A. A. (2003). *The minds of marginalized Black men: Making sense of mobility, opportunity, and future life chances.* Princeton, NJ: Princeton University Press.

CHAPTER 8

The Heart of the Matter

Recruitment and Training of MDP Instructors

Jerome Gourdine

The Manhood Development Program (MDP) within the African American Male Achievement (AAMA) initiative takes a unique approach to recruiting and training course facilitators. To provide some context, I'll begin with the story of a very special king,[1] Darryl Aikins, whom we affectionately knew as "Boobie." He represents our North Star—the kind of young man the Manhood Development Program courses are designed to produce and the kind of instructors we hope to recruit—the reason why I do the work that I do, and even the model I look to for the way I live my life.

While a sophomore in high school and a standout football star, Boobie went to the hospital for a bad cough, and, after several tests, he was informed that he had leukemia. For many young men this would have been a reason to give up, or turn inward, expecting sympathy and a free pass out of hard work. But from the moment Boobie was told of the diagnosis, and throughout the ensuing blood transfusions, hospital stays, and chemotherapy, he never complained about his health. He never asked for sympathy. When asked how he could maintain such a positive attitude, even with everything he was going through, his response was, "I'm alive today." He focused on setting goals; he was determined to beat the cancer and play football again. He accomplished the latter goal, helping his team win the championship that year. Unfortunately, Boobie was not able to beat the cancer, and when that became undeniable, Boobie's new goal was to graduate from high school. He made it to his senior year, and despite the doctors telling him a few times during the fall that he had only a couple of days to live, he beat their prognosis, and that spring he walked across the stage to receive his diploma. Just three weeks after this important milestone in Boobie's life, he transitioned in 2017.

During the celebration of Boobie's life, community members and family used powerful words to describe his character and a life well lived, even if it was only for 18 years. He was described as determined, goal-oriented, purpose-driven, community-driven, resilient, and joyful. Above all, the one word consistently used to describe this young man by everyone who encountered him during his life was *love*—the people in his life felt his love.

I share this story because the character Boobie displayed during his battle with leukemia is the character model we expect of ourselves and of our facilitators in working with the kings. The goal for all of us is to be or become the type of person Boobie became: goal-oriented, purpose-driven, community-driven, and above all, love-driven. This is what we have in mind when we recruit and train our future facilitators. We honor Boobie's memory with our work in AAMA and the Manhood Development Program.

My journey to AAMA and the Manhood Development Program, of which I'm currently the Director, began in 2012. I was a middle school principal in Oakland, and one day while I was standing on the stairs outside my school watching my students go home for the day, the former OUSD superintendent, Dr. Anthony Smith, approached me. Acknowledging the culture I'd developed at the school and in the wider community, he told me he wanted to offer me an opportunity to spread the same positive atmosphere across the district. He explained that in order to do so, I'd have to leave my position as principal and move downtown to the central office in the following school year.

To be honest, it took some time for me to accept the opportunity. As a middle school educator, I enjoyed a tremendous amount of success, especially as a principal. I had been named one of the 25 most influential principals in the country. I also had the privilege of having two of my teachers named as California Teachers of the Year. Six of my assistant principals were promoted to principal, and other certificated and classified staff won numerous awards at the district level. And beyond that, Dr. Smith was right: I had created a community at my school that I was deeply connected and committed to.

At the same time, even with all of those accomplishments, I always knew something was missing. This was based on the knowledge that certain student populations, especially African American males, were still not succeeding to the same degree as other student populations at my school. African American males were too often the population sent to the office for disciplinary reasons, and often remained disconnected from school. I felt incomplete and unfulfilled as an educator knowing that African American males, the group of students I personally belonged to and represented, were not as successful as the other groups of students at my school. I often thought of Boobie, and wondered if there was a way I could have a bigger impact in inspiring more of the kings at my school to emulate the way he was living his life.

As the superintendent and I continued to talk about the possibilities of future positions, he asked where I saw myself being best positioned to have a positive effect district-wide, and I told him that if I was going to leave my school, the place I could see myself was with the office of African American Male Achievement (AAMA). After years of seeing and participating in the work Executive Director Christopher Chatmon was doing with the kings in AAMA, and knowing Chris both personally and professionally, when I was offered the opportunity of a leadership position alongside him I decided to make the move. This transition in 2012 marked the beginning of my life's work.

Chris Chatmon frames our task in AAMA as creating a movement to interrupt the current educational system that our kings experience. He realized that in order to effectively respond to the needs of the African American males in OUSD, we had to get a deep and clear understanding of what they were experiencing, and what they felt would make school a more positive experience for them. In order to do that, we conducted a listening campaign when AAMA was first established, and we started out by going from school to school to learn from the students themselves. The feedback we got from the listening campaign was essential in creating the Manhood Development Program, and in establishing the concept of *agape*—the highest form of brotherly love—as the guide for everything we do.

We recognize that the core of that effort lies in our ability to surround our kings with classroom facilitators who are the highest-quality people we can find. They need complete freedom of thought, a strong understanding of and respect for our cultural background and history, and the knowledge of how that connects to being an African American male today. They need not only to have an understanding of the challenges we face, but also an asset-based rather than deficit-based mindset, and a desire to be a positive force for change. We look for men who show a willingness and desire to be a lifelong learner, who believe in collaboration and teamwork. Above all, they have to have a demonstrable love for Black boys.

Knowing the kinds of relationships I'd developed with students and faculty, and the recruitment and retention I'd achieved as a middle school principal, when I came to AAMA, Chris Chatmon gave me responsibility for the recruitment of AAMA facilitators. This also required that I establish the framework for their training, to ensure that once they were brought into the program they would have the necessary systems and support to become the kind of high-quality facilitators our program demands.

SELECTING "DIFFERENT" INSTRUCTORS

A theme we consistently use as a framework in AAMA is the notion of *being different*. In that spirit, I recognized early on that the process of recruiting and training our facilitators needed to be different from the traditional process I was accustomed to as a principal. In order to place the right facilitator in front of our kings, someone who can effectively reach and educate them, I have to make sure they possess certain qualities and characteristics beyond, or different from, the characteristics we might have looked for in traditional classroom teachers. Even our process of interviewing and vetting had to be different from the traditional process.

One of the first major, nontraditional practices we established in the recruitment process was having an informal meeting with a candidate before a formal interview is initiated. This means that after reading a résumé that gives us a sense of a good possibility, we try to meet the candidate at a neutral location to just get a take on him as a person, and this can be a pretty intuitive process. Our goal here is to assess his interest in the position, and to gauge the fit between a candidate, his goals and motivations, the objectives of our program, and the larger movement to love Black boys that our program is a part of. This provides a measure of whether or not we want to move forward with scheduling a more formal interview.

Once we've chosen a candidate for a formal interview, rather than a one-on-one interview we try to organize a group of leaders and AAMA kings to participate in the process, with questions geared toward the candidate's level of knowledge and experience working with African American male students in a variety of settings, from elementary to high school. During the group interview, we want our kings to be able to get to know the candidate alongside us, to let us know whether they feel a sense of real connection, since these are the young men the facilitator will eventually be working with. As an aside, this also gives our kings a real-life opportunity to see and participate in the hiring process.

Our major philosophy for recruiting is that *we hire for will and train for skill*. During interviews, our intention is to assess a candidate's level of love for and commitment to the community, the personal resources he possesses, and what he can contribute to the organization. We look for men who express and demonstrate the desire to work in a community as a member of that community, and the willingness to take the stance of being a lifelong learner with respect to improving himself and our community.

Primarily, we look for candidates who show a true desire to engage, encourage, and empower our kings. This might come through, for example, in the way they respond to a scenario of a discipline issue we create. We listen for the candidate's recognition that a student's behavior isn't "who they are" but the way they acted in that moment. We want to hear them express the mindset that despite a king's behavior, they will know or be willing to consider multiple ways of continuing to engage, giving the king multiple opportunities to learn. But unapologetically, our bottom line is this: If the candidate does not see the need to love each of our kings as if he were his own child, this is not the organization for him. This is a top priority in our recruiting process—love! This is what's at the heart of the matter.

Beyond establishing the candidate's love-driven commitment to the community, the interview questions we've created are also intended to raise a number of issues with respect to the candidate's ability to adapt to new environments, and his ability to support resilience for students and their families. Other questions assess the candidate's ability to adapt to unexpected situations while working in a school environment, such as working with teachers and adults who don't believe in the movement around supporting Black boys. Given that possibility, we're looking for advocacy skills and the awareness of the *need* to advocate for Black boys. We'd like to know that the candidate is a person who can influence other teachers and staff members, building relationships not just with the kings, but with the whole community—teachers, parents, and families—in order to create cultural change.

ALTERNATIVE CREDENTIALING PROCESS

Many of our facilitators don't come into the organization as teachers, but are men who have exemplified a connection to their community primarily through youth development. But in the first years of the program, we struggled to find a path for these candidates into the classroom. In order to recruit and employ nontraditional candidates, we had to come up with a creative solution to the roadblock created by the traditional credentialing process. Our answer was to offer our candidates the opportunity to earn a Designated Subjects Career Technical Education Teaching Credential in Education, Child Development, and Family Services, and this has proved to be a real asset to the program. The CTE credentialing program at UC Berkeley Extension allows us to recruit candidates from the community who have experience working with youth and families in a variety of different areas, but don't have a formal credential. Through AAMA we can assist them with applying for and enrolling in the CTE credential program, a 3-year process in which the facilitator takes classes to fulfill the credentialing requirements, while also facilitating classes with AAMA. The credential program offers another level of support to the facilitators, and five of our facilitators have now completed their credential.

TRAINING

Because we *hire for will and train for skill*, we've created an extensive training process for our facilitators, which we prefer to describe more as a development process. It's an educational process that helps the facilitators mobilize and hone the love they have for students into effective pedagogy. In our training process, and throughout the work we do at AAMA, we work as a community of African American male educators to model how to transform love for young Black men into effective practices that produce quantifiable results.

This first part of our training is a week-long program, 40 hours of intensive training in the principles and pedagogy that are unique to AAMA. All members of the AAMA leadership participate in the trainings, but our curriculum specialist, Baayan Bakari, and our program manager and the first Manhood Development teacher in AAMA, Jahi, are the main trainers, along with a few others who bring different resources to the training program.

One of the first and fundamental steps in our training program is to engage the facilitators in the principle of brotherhood, and by doing so we create brotherhood. It's a different experience than most people have been through in teacher training, and those who have experienced it will tell you they walked away with a new sense of brotherhood. We stress the importance of routines and rituals, such as a handshake and eye contact whenever we meet—we never enter a room without acknowledging each other. Our routines continue throughout the training, so that our sessions always have a recognizable beginning, middle, and end. A greeting to begin, when we acknowledge one another and check in, a clear agenda and goal to focus the middle, and an end that connects us, a ritual that brings us all together and acknowledges our brotherhood, such as seven *harambes,* or calls for unity and working together.

Although I'd like to have the training last even longer, we get through quite a long list of topics during the week, ranging from literacy to academic discourse, pedagogical strategies, teaching modalities, lesson sharing and facilitating, unit and lesson planning, character development, collaborative planning, and engaging the kings in the learning process.

Utilizing the concept of collective genius, the framework of our facilitator development trainings posits that all voices are equal and equitable. Our goal is to establish our brotherhood as a knowledge-building community, because we know our facilitators come to us with strengths we need and knowledge we need; therefore we incorporate the voices and experiences of our facilitators throughout the process. It isn't simply a one-way street where we're filling empty vessels; we role-model the type of facilitation we expect of them by engaging in professional development that draws on the best practices from each person in the classroom. We don't just teach; we listen and create relationships, because relationships are key.

THE KHEPERA CURRICULUM

The basis of the content for the Manhood Development classes is the Khepera curriculum. Our curriculum specialist, Baayan Bakari, developed the curriculum and is instrumental in supporting the facilitators during the training and throughout the year in implementing the curriculum in the classroom. This is a culturally relevant curriculum created specifically for students of color, and during the week we cover the core of the curriculum, which focuses on identity development and engages students in an exploration of the forces that impact different cultural groups in society. Through engaging in the curriculum first as learners, the facilitators often come to a new or deeper understanding of the concepts they'll be exploring with the kings in the classroom. Again, it's a modeling process, and an engagement process that we all benefit from.

By the end of the week we've covered a lot of material, but our training continues throughout the year.

ONGOING PROFESSIONAL DEVELOPMENT

In addition to the training week, the AAMA administrative team visits and supports the facilitators at their respective school sites throughout the school year, and this is one of my roles. I'm focused more on supporting the school administrative team and the staff at the high schools where we're working, and Jahi is focused on the elementary and middle schools. The goal is to spend time with all of the facilitators at all of the sites, especially while they're teaching, and in addition to the documentation and feedback that AAMA in-house researcher Gerald Williams provides on a regular basis, the facilitators have monthly narratives they have to complete. While we're on-site our interactions can take various forms, such as providing feedback to a lesson, modeling a lesson, substituting for a facilitator if needed, or providing resources to the facilitator or students and their families. The facilitators enrolled in the CTE program at Berkeley are also required to observe and be observed, so in that case we follow a state-mandated protocol that requires us to observe them in the classroom, and then write an evaluation using state standards. But staying outside of the traditional framework means that our support for facilitators might also entail calling them to see how they're doing, and having a brother-to-brother check-in to ensure they know we care about them and are invested in their success.

Besides the on-site observations and feedback, every other week we have AAMA professional learning community meetings that cover a range of topics, but always begin with a brotherhood check-in, where we ask the facilitators how they're feeling, what's going on, and if they have something they want to lift up, or share, for whatever reason. By doing this we continue to build the camaraderie that allows us to connect and provide advice and resources. The main part of the Learning Community meetings focuses on ways of implementing the curriculum, but we also frequently discuss the relationship-building that the facilitators are involved in, because the relationships are everything. If they're not building relationships with their kings, they're not doing the work.

On the logistical side, during the bimonthly meetings we also discuss the day-to-day issues like the school calendar and special events, for example the Manhood Development Conference. This is an annual event where we have kings from all over the Bay Area join us. We ensure all are made aware of the role and expectations we have for them. Sometimes facilitators are given the assignment to facilitate a portion of the meeting, which gives them an opportunity to share a practice with the rest of us, and gain experience in professional development too. In fact, we recently had a facilitator share with us that he's having his kings teach the class now—that he's transferred the concept of collective genius to his classroom, giving his kings the opportunity to share their own knowledge with their peers. It's powerful what we can learn from one another by holding one another up and listening this way. At the end of the Learning Community meeting we conclude with a ritual that brings us all together, acknowledging our brotherhood and our shared work.

SELF-CARE

The most recent component we've added to our training and support system comes from the realization that our facilitators need to understand and practice self-care when working with our kings. We expect a lot from them, and although it can be incredibly rewarding, they're engaged in an extremely challenging process. To meet the need for self-care practices, we engaged Asar Tfehai, a specialist in natural healing, to conduct a workshop with the facilitators in training, and established an additional meeting every other month focused on healing strategies for the facilitators. The topics covered in this class range from proper nutrition, exercise, sleep, and meditation, to ways of coping when dealing with trauma and conflict. We know that this is an important practice for all of us, and one that also aligns with our love-driven mission. We have to know how to love and care for ourselves in order to do it for others.

This work isn't just a job, by any means. It's about being part of a movement that we're all committed to and inspired by. We're creating major cultural change through bringing a powerful brotherhood of positive, goal-oriented, purpose-driven, community-driven, and love-driven men into our schools so that more of us can carry out Darryl (Boobie) Aikins's legacy.

NOTE

1. "King" is used in the context of MDP courses to affirm students; it is an intentional negation of hegemonic stereotypical narratives imposed upon young Black males through popular images and through their treatment in schools.

CHAPTER 9

Ties That Bind

Forging Black Girl Space in the Black (Male) Educational "Crisis"

kihana miraya ross

As the mother of two Black teenage daughters, I often lamented the lack of Black television options available to them throughout their childhood. The kinds of shows I grew up watching simply didn't exist anymore. As a result, I relied heavily on channels like TV One, which played reruns of old shows such as *A Different World, Fresh Prince of Bel-Air, Family Matters*, and so forth. Hence, while many would argue Black television has recently made a strong comeback, much of the Black television my children watched growing up (when Black TV was at an all-time low) were repeats of these older shows. Watching these shows together served to expose my daughters to television images where we were reflected in positive ways, and also allowed me to reminisce about the "good old days" when nuanced visions of blackness were commonplace in television.

Recently, we all watched an episode of *Moesha* together entitled "The Million Boy March." *Moesha* was a popular 1990s television show starring singer and actress Brandy as a teenage Black girl growing up in the Leimert Park area of Los Angeles. In this particular episode, Moesha begins the show with a voiceover that says, "When it comes to giving women our proper respect, why do some guys still act like they're clueless?" We soon learn that the "guys" Moesha refers to are members of a youth organization for Black boys, the Council for Concerned Youth (CCY). The CCY contacts Moesha's church, where the congregation is primarily Black girls, to inform them of a scholarship competition for Black boys. Moesha, incensed that the scholarship isn't open to Black girls, crashes the group's meeting and demands to be included in the fundraiser planning process and demands that the scholarship be made available to Black girls as well. After much protest from the group, Moesha successfully joins, but doesn't quite receive the warmest welcome. For example, the Black male leader of the group says to Moesha,

"Why can't the Black woman just support the Black man? Instead of always jumping up in his face tryna tear him down?"

As the story unfolds, Moesha clearly outperforms her male counterparts in organizing and even gets the then popular music group Jodeci to perform; Moesha becomes the primary force behind the event's success. Still, when the media comes to take a picture for the newspaper, the male leader of the group asks Moesha to refrain from being in the photo: "I think the world needs to see that this is the work of young Black brothers." Moesha responds, "even if it's not?" In traditional sitcom-ending form, a few moments later all of the boys encourage Moesha to be a part of the photo and they smile happily together for a picture. The show ends with the photo and the newspaper headline: "Million Boys Led by One in a Million Girl."

I begin with this vignette because it's an excellent entry point into an often difficult conversation: Does talking about the needs of Black girls signal a problem with programs designed exclusively for Black boys? Does having programs for Black boys necessarily diminish the very real struggles Black girls face in every facet of the education system? What role might patriarchy play in the focus on Black males that has galvanized media and research attention? Why can't we just have (as Moesha wanted) a program that is open to both Black girls and Black boys? These are profound questions and become particularly significant in the context of a district-sponsored manhood development program for Black boys, and the absence of a similar district initiative available to Black girls.[1]

If we begin to think about these questions through the lens of Moesha, we may understand that her anger with the exclusion of Black girls signals a pushback against the ways Black girls (and their needs) are often left out of the conversation completely. Further, the show is written in a way that demonstrates that Moesha is needed in this boy's group and, in fact, she achieves things for the group they would not have been able to achieve on their own. Hence, the message is not only that Black girls should be allowed in this space, but rather, Black girls (and women) play a critical role in the success of Black boys (and men) and the Black community more broadly. In recognizing that Black women are often positioned as what Zora Neale Hurston (1937/2008) referred to as the "mule of de world," this episode attempts to problematize the heavy focus on the needs of Black boys to the exclusion of Black girls.

While this episode aired in the early 1990s, in our current historical moment when there are exclusive programs the focus of these race-specific projects still tends to be on Black boys. Even on a national level, programs like My Brother's Keeper, an initiative of the Obama administration, aimed to address the opportunity gaps faced by boys and young men of color.

While this work is a critical component of supporting a broader agenda of educational equity, it can also inadvertently obscure the violence of the racialized experiences Black girls have in school. In fact, in response to the announcement of My Brother's Keeper, Kimberlé Crenshaw spearheaded an open letter, signed by thousands of influential women of color, calling on Obama to "re-align this important initiative to reflect the values of inclusion, equal opportunity and shared fate that have propelled our historic struggle for racial justice forward" (Henderson, 2014). The problem, however, is not that there is something inherently wrong with a focus on programs designed exclusively for Black boys. Rather, it's the absence of a focus and corresponding opportunities available for Black girls. In other words, addressing the specific needs of Black girls shouldn't inherently diminish the important work being done to serve the specific needs of Black boys. So while Moesha offers an important critique about the lack of focus on Black girls, the way the show is written creates an unnecessary dissonance between the championing of Black girls and spaces that are racially and gender exclusive. Perhaps if the resources existed, Moesha would have advocated for a scholarship for Black girls *specifically*—or pushed for the creation of a concerned youth council for Black girls. This would also have prevented the show from having to choose sides. In the end, as opposed to celebrating the success of an organization for Black boys, if we remember the headline of the newspaper coverage ("Million Boys Led by One in a Million Girl"), we leave with the idea that the group wouldn't have accomplished anything without a Black girl (Moesha). I want to offer an alternative ending. What if this Black boys organization successfully organized their fundraiser on their own? What if, also, Moesha articulated the injustice in the lack of opportunities and resources for Black girls and pushed for a similar structure for Black girls? What if the show became a critique of the idea that Black girls should have to fight for the kinds of supports more readily developed for Black boys? What if the show aimed to resist the narrative that Black girls are alright (Crenshaw, Ocen, & Nanda, 2015), undeserving, or even invisible, and instead illuminated the notion that while there are certain experiences shared by Black people en masse, regardless of sex, gender, sexual orientation, ability, income level, and so forth, there are also numerous and varying Black intersectional identities and experiences that deserve their own attention to specificity (Dumas & ross, 2016)?

While scholars, public intellectuals, and even musical artists (see, for example, Beyoncé's *Lemonade*) have begun to highlight the obstacles facing Black girls and women more broadly, the experiences of Black girls in schools remain sadly underexplored. Still, in the existing literature, scholars have noted the ways, for example, that Black girls may be perceived as more defiant, loud, and unladylike than their non-Black counterparts (Morris, 2007). Perhaps as a result of these perceptions, and in direct response to the increasing attention on the racialized disciplining of Black boys, scholars have also began to interrogate the disproportionate discipline rates of Black girls in schools, noting the relative risk for disciplinary action is higher for Black girls when compared to their White counterparts than for Black boys when compared to their White counterparts (Crenshaw et al., 2015). Still, the Black educational "crisis" is often understood as a Black *male* crisis, and likewise, critical interventions are often conceptualized with the Black male in mind. Perhaps, as Ayana Brown suggests, for "those 'loud black girls,' we must continue to consider and respond to *why* they speak so loudly. We must question not only the volume of their speech but also the substance of their concerns. How do we regard these girls who have been dismissed or *trained* to be resilient through silence" (Brown, 2011).

In this chapter I want to highlight an exclusively Black-girl space and underscore various issues facing Black girls in schools *specifically*. Pushing back against the "single story" (Adichie, 2009) of the Jezebel, hypermasculine, unsophisticated, angry, defiant, disruptive, loud Black girl, this chapter reflects on an ethnographic case study that explores both the ways Black girls are racialized and hypersexualized in schools. I utilize the concept of *Black Girl Space*, which refers to the space in the margins that Black girls and women produce to enact educational fugitivity. The production of such Black Girl Space facilitates a reimagining of a Black girl identity, and the development of a radical Black subjectivity. At the same time, I also highlight the synergy between the pedagogical philosophies and practices of the MDP instructors and that of the Black woman instructor of this space. In doing so, I draw our attention to the ways these critical educators demonstrate an awareness of the needs of Black students more broadly, and also the ways these instructors leverage a shared racial and gendered identity to facilitate students' awareness of different modes of navigating common struggles. Still, I want to problematize the notion that shared racial and gender characteristics automatically lend themselves to positive teacher-student relationships. Like many of the MDP instructors, this particular teacher's frames, philosophies, and theories, in conjunction with her shared communal history with her students, are what allowed for the kind of liberatory Black educational project explored in this study. Moreover, this instructor's positionality as a Black woman who lived in the same community as her students privileged her within this context.

WOMEN'S STUDIES AT JEFFERSON HIGH

The class referenced in this study was formally called a women's studies course and took place at Jefferson High School,[2] a public high school in a large city in the San Francisco Bay Area. While the Manhood Development Program was a formal district initiative, this exclusively Black women's studies class at the time was an anomaly. Ms. C, the course instructor, was asked to create a space for Black girls as a result of increasing disciplinary incidents involving Black girls at the high school level. While Ms. C was initially hesitant, fearing she could not count on the administration for the support she needed, in the end she agreed to teach the course every day—one class during fifth period and one during sixth period.

The course was presented to Black girls (grades 9–12) as a women's studies class (for which they would receive elective credit), and girls were encouraged, but not required, to participate. The course's curriculum was designed to address student needs across a variety of domains—physical, emotional, academic, and social. It was aimed at encouraging students to learn more about themselves, their cultural and racial history, and their communities with the goal of helping them think more expansively about Black girlhood. Class activities centered around discussions of contemporary issues; critical analysis of popular media like songs and movies; discussion about race, gender, sex and sexuality, complexion, hair, security guards, police, sexual harassment, love and relationships; and so forth. Finally, many classes centered on the needs of the girls in the class on that particular day, and curriculum was always fluid when and where necessary.

As a result of administrative turnover, the principal who asked Ms. C to develop the course was no longer at the school as the fall approached. Fearing even less structural support, Ms. C limited the course to 10 students per period (or 20 students total). While each class was initially full, by the end of the first semester, there were 12 students remaining. Those 12 students remained in the course for the entirety of the second semester. Importantly, of the 8 girls who dropped the course, 7 did so as a result of no longer being a student in the school. Two of the students moved out of the city altogether, citing safety concerns. The one student who remained in the school but not in the course dropped the course very early on. After stealing from multiple girls in the space, and also sharing confidential information with students outside of the class, she felt unwelcomed (by the other girls) to return. All 12 remaining girls identified as Black or African American, and all identified with the "she" pronoun. The girls ranged in their complexions and sizes, from particularly thin to overweight—from a deep dark chocolate to a lighter caramel.

MS. C

Ms. C was a petite Black woman with a caramel complexion and an infectious smile. She would often dress in clothes that signaled her connection to youth culture, mixing in her own Afrocentric flair. She had also begun the process of locking her hair (developing dreadlocks), interestingly, as opposed to cutting her hair and beginning with short twists (as many people do); she decided to begin the process with her shoulder length, curly (but not quite kinky) hair. I signal this only because for many months, it was unclear what she was doing with her hair; this became a recurring point of conversation between Ms. C and the girls in the class. The general consensus was that she was "ruining" her hair and should cease with the dreadlocks business immediately! She would sometimes wrap her hair in a headwrap or pull it back into a ponytail. She had a few different pairs of glasses, each one with its own quirky shape or pattern. Her nose was pierced with a small gold hoop and she often wore large, dramatic earrings. Overall, she presented as a healthy mix of Afrocentric, urban, and quirky.

Ms. C was in graduate school at the time, completing her master's in women's spirituality, a program that combined gender/women's studies, ethnic studies, philosophy, social justice, and spirituality. Prior to her role as the instructor for the women's studies course, she was an English teacher at Jefferson High School for one year. Prior to that, she taught English/literature for 7 years at two other public high schools in the Bay Area. Ms. C took extreme pride in being a teacher, and she understood the work she did with students as necessarily always extending beyond the classroom. Still, she was always in her classroom long before I arrived, and she always left hours after the bell rang.

Like many of the MDP instructors, Ms. C understood that the ways Black students experienced anti-Blackness in schools necessitated creating a space that would serve as a refuge from the larger school. This often meant that she positioned herself *with* her students and *against* the administration. In the areas of discipline, conflict resolution, and the power of words, for example, there is a strong parity between the philosophies and pedagogical practices of Ms. C and those of many of the MDP instructors.

ON DISCIPLINE

More than disassociating from the school administration, Ms. C had to wrestle with the collateral damage of the adults in the school creating an unsafe disciplinary environment. Already, the way the space was constructed ensured that student behaviors that would be disciplined in other spaces within the school were either not considered a discipline issue, or rather were praised within this Black girls' space. In the beginning, Ms. C decided to enact discipline outside of the classroom space so as to minimize the chances of triggering students accustomed to unfair and inappropriate interactions with the larger school staff. Still, there were moments when Ms. C determined it was impossible to avoid direct confrontation within the space. I asked her about her policy on sending students out of the classroom:

> Ms. C: To me, that's a last resort, last last last last LAST resort.
> Interviewer: Did you ever do it?
> Ms. C: Timone.
> Interviewer: She got a referral?
> Ms. C: No, I didn't write no referral. I never wrote a referral because, again, I felt like, if I'm sending you to someone then that defeats my purpose and this is bad, but I tell other teachers, like, that's just me, but use your mind. Other teachers will be like, "The principal didn't help me; he made it worse!" and I'm like, "Well why did you send them to him? If you see that it doesn't work, why do you keep doing it?" So I'm like, I don't send them to him because I know it's just going to make it worse and counterproductive to my values and rules. So if I felt like the office was a place where discipline and restorative justice happened, I would've sent them, possibly . . .

For Ms. C, sending students to the principal would make the situation "worse" and be "counterproductive to [her] values and rules." This is a critical distinction. In other words, more than the necessity of positioning herself as an ally and advocate of students, in opposition to the administration, Ms. C firmly believed that sending students to the office would actually make whatever situation deemed potentially discipline-worthy, worse. In fact, she does not believe "discipline" happens in the office. When she indicates that if she believed this were the case she would likely send students there, she implies that if she understood the administration as partners in resisting anti-Blackness, she would also partner with them in healthy and effective disciplining of Black girls. Still, when she indicates "possibly" at the end of her sentence, she signals her view of the impossibility of such a partnership.

Beyond her refusal to send students to the formal disciplinary body within the school, as a general rule Ms. C refused to send students out of the classroom. Centering the students' well-being, she questions:

> This is my thing, where am I sending them to? I'm sending them to go hang out on that corner. I'm sending them to go buy chips. I'm sending them in front. That's terrible. What? No! So that's why, again, I was always like, I'll talk to them in class, before class, after, really try to bring the point home, give them opportunities to really show up differently . . . in this climate, keeping them in is more powerful.

Sending students out of this space is also counterproductive to Ms. C's values and rules, and ultimately, her philosophy. As she imagines what she may be sending students to if she asks them to leave, she recognizes the senselessness of sending students to the very things she aims to protect them from. Further, given the various forms of #BlackGirlMagic happening within the classroom,[3] keeping students inside is always "more powerful."

CONFLICT RESOLUTION

Ms. C's discipline practices were another way she enacted conflict resolution as a pedagogical tool within the classroom. When asked about the ways Ms. C disciplined them, all students indicated that Ms. C was committed to working through problems in a way that was different from other teachers' approaches. In comparing other teachers to Ms. C, one student commented, "they be so quick to just you know kick you outta class and don't really care about you know you stayin or tryin to make it—like, try to fix it and stuff like that. So yeah." Another student noted, "She discipline us by gettin on our level you know and tryin to make stuff work and tryin to fix it rather to other teachers they don't care they just write a referral and just send us to the principal or somewhere else so they could fix it when that's really not the problem you know." Hence, Ms. C's mode of disciplining was inseparable from her commitment to resolve any and all conflicts in the space, whether they were between students or between a student and herself. In contrast to the ways students experienced other teachers as uncaring or unwilling to care enough to resolve an issue, they appreciated Ms. C's dedication to reinforcing Black girl humanity, and maintaining a healthy space.

WORDS MATTER

As noted earlier, Ms. C was keenly aware of the ways society produces and reproduces harmful racialized notions of Black girl identity. Hence, Ms. C was very deliberate: She consistently provided the girls with positive reinforcement and did not permit the degradation of Black girls and women in the space. For example, at the beginning of the year, most of the girls referred to one another and to Black girls outside of the class as "bitch." While not employing a zero tolerance policy for the word, Ms. C worked with the girls to think about what it meant to define themselves in that way. By the end of the course, she noted a marked difference in the way girls were employing the word:

> And so even though terms like that still show up in my classroom,
> I feel like I noticed a shift with it, I definitely noticed a shift with it,
> um, where they're more apt to, it's not the only word they use. They
> might use that word, but they also might use different things like
> woman or girl, or they're already expanding what that means, or
> even just how they relate to it. I felt like, at the beginning of the year
> they were using that word more as an identity descriptor and now I
> felt like they were using it as more of what it really is, as an insult.
> You know what I mean, so what does it mean to have an insult be
> how you define your identity?

Thus while the term was still used to levy an insult during a story or in the
context of talking about a teacher or administrator someone felt wronged
by, they were no longer hailing each other as "bitches."

While Ms. C was working with her Black girl students on reframing how they identified one another, so too were MDP instructors with their Black boy students. Many instructors insisted that boys not us the "n word" in their classrooms, and even offered alternative descriptors such as "brotha" or "king." While the n word is attached to a more obvious highly racialized and violent history, the "b word" has particular gendered and racialized connotations when levied against Black girls and women. Both Ms. C and MDP instructors worked with their students to refrain from referring to their male or female counterparts in these terms as well. In other words, in both boy and girl spaces, educators were working toward a moratorium on the use of the "n word" and the "b word."

Similarly, the discipline philosophy and practices Ms. C employed in her classroom closely mirror the pedagogical choices of many of the MDP instructors. Ms. C and MDP instructors shared ideas such as reframing what counts as a disciplinary moment, or refusing to send students to the office (even if they sent students out of the classroom). In these instances, regardless of whether the space was created for Black boys or Black girls, these philosophies and practices are rooted in these critical Black educators' understanding of the schools' disciplinary structures as inherently anti-Black. In fact, in both spaces, their approach to discipline essentially began with their disapproval of the ways adults in the school interact with children and the ways those interactions inform students' understanding of what it means to be disciplined.

BLACK GIRL BEGINNINGS

While there was significant ideological and pedagogical overlap in Ms. C's class and the MDP classes, there were also marked points of departure that highlight the importance of separate spaces that attend to students' intersectional identities. For example, given that Black girls must consistently negotiate their existence in a school and society where their skin tone, hair texture, and physical features are positioned in opposition to an aesthetic ideal, there was a symbolic (and sometimes literal) violent response to being in an exclusively Black-girl space. Ms. C notes:

> In the first two months of school, every week had two or three major conflicts between people that were just like, "I refuse to be in the same room as her" or "Imma rip her head off," and all of this really violent . . . almost like they were just raging at each other, and coming into this room together. It was like, you know, when you try to put magnets together and they're the opposite side, it was like that. Like, that's how absolutely vicious the self-hate was, and I felt overwhelmed every single day because of the things I said before about not having the support and those other, you know, and the way this space is so different than other spaces. And if I had kind of just had a, you know, hard line, I run the risk of losing all of them, but at the same time, that can't happen. So I had times, I did a lot of mediating, and I was like, vent to me and get it all out so that you don't go and fight homegirl because it's not worth it. Like, tell me what's really going on. So I had to take a lot of that and listen to a lot of . . . you know in the cartoons, like when the hair's flowing back [laughs]. Really just strengthening myself, so then having the mediations, and that was before Sista Latifah was here. And my little ass, I'm trying to sit people down, and talk to them, and make sure, like, you ain't gonna jump on her and [it was] RIDICULOUS!

I share Ms. C's words here to illustrate the significance of what it means to create, develop, and produce Black space together. That is, you cannot simply put Black people together and wait for a Black liberatory experience. Rather, Black space in this context is purposefully constructed (and often contested) by all actors within the space. In the beginning of the year, the same kinds of interactions Black girls were having with one another outside of this class were explicitly present within it. Further, Ms. C suspects that the fact that the space was all Black may have actually increased the tension. She notes:

> I actually feel like if it was mixed race, I actually think there would've been less conflict, which is ironic because people think about racial beef amongst students, but I actually feel like they're really comfortable being in mixed classes because they're in that all

the time. So when you make it all Black, the self-hate, it comes up real BIG. Like, the internalized stuff, it really comes up because your sister sitting next to you is your reflection and everything you're uncomfortable in yourself, it's in your face for a whole hour. So some really intense dynamics came up.

According to Ms. C, being in a classroom with all Black girls forced the students to confront their own self-hatred in the context of an anti-Black world. While in other work, my colleagues and I have discussed the comfort Black boys described feeling in all-Black spaces (see for example, Givens et al., 2016; Nasir et al., 2013; ross et al., 2016), Ms. C asserts that in this context, the opposite was initially true. This analysis is supported by the ways Black girls themselves described their original feelings about being in an exclusively Black-girl class and the ways they felt about Black girls overall.

When asked how they felt about having a class with all Black girls, all respondents reported being concerned that the class would be a negative experience as a result of bringing Black girls together. Shaunté explains,

> *Shaunté:* To be honest at first I thought, like, oh my gosh, like, this gonna be hecka messy. Like, there's gonna be hecka drama and hecka stuff like that, but it turned out to actually be a very good moment.
> *Interviewer:* Why did you think it was gonna be messy at first?
> *Shaunté:* Cuz it was just like, I don't know, like, just a class full of Black girls, so I'm just like, oh my gosh, like.

Other students commented, "at first, I'm thinkin, like, its gone be a riot in dis class" or "all these girls gone be ratchet and stuff" or "all I know is Imma end up slappin somebody. I don't care, you look at me the wrong way Imma slap you" or "all Black females is not gon work." Additionally, it was not uncommon for students to make comments that denigrated Black girls more generally. Statements such as "bum bitches do bum things" or "bitches with raggedy purses don't care about shit," for example, were a painful reminder of the ways Black girls were perceiving and rearticulating negative societal images of themselves. Although students reported feeling markedly different as the year progressed, in order to understand how Black girls reimagine Blackness, it becomes critical to consider where Black girls *begin* with one another; this starting point, while often overlooked, renders the kinds of transformative positioning occurring in these spaces all the more meaningful.

BLACK GIRL HYPERSEXUALIZED

In addition to the initial struggles Black girls had with one another, they also discussed what it meant to be a Black girl in particular—an experience often markedly different from that of their male counterparts. For example, many class conversations spanned what it meant to be a Black girl at Jefferson and the various ways girls felt sexually harassed at the school. Particularly during extremely hot spells, girls struggled with wearing something that kept them cool but also didn't create a space where they would receive unwanted attention from boys. While these conversations were mostly around things boys would say to them (i.e., "look at all that ass" or "ratchet" or "can I touch it?"), there were also instances where both male and female administrators made comments to girls that made the girls uncomfortable. For example, one day Daronda came to class upset at the way a White female administrator indicated her shirt was too revealing. Daronda noted the administrator said, "You're blessed in a way that I'm not so I'm gonna need you to cover those." During our interview, Laquita discussed a time a male administrator indicated her shirt was too revealing:

> I was—actually, it was a principal, actually. It was Mr. James. I was in the cafeteria sitting there eating my food, and he came and sat with us, and then I had my shirt, my shirt was down, but I didn't know it was down. Nobody was saying nun so I didn't know. And he came up to me and was like, "why yo chest all out like that, you need to put them thangs up," and I was like, why are you looking at me that kind of way, and I was uncomfortable. And I didn't have no jacket, so I couldn't just, like, cover up, I was, like, stuck so I'm just like, wow. And everybody was just like, did he really just say dat to you? He had said somethin else, I forgot what he had said, and I was just like, you are our principal. You are a grown man who has kids our age probably, and you sayin stuff like this. That's not coo.

Beyond the regular sexual harassment girls reported hearing from boys in their school, both Daronda and Laquita are also forced to navigate inappropriate language from school administrators. While they both felt uncomfortable in the situations, neither girl felt like there was any possible resolution. Rather, these kinds of situations are simply another aspect of schooling Black girls must endure.

More than verbal assaults, girls also discussed instances in which they were touched inappropriately. The following excerpt from field notes represents one such example.

I notice that Dalesha is not here today. I asked Ms. C why Dalesha
was absent and she indicated that apparently Dalesha had on very
short shorts because it was extremely hot today. Dalesha left early
because she was upset because boys kept slapping and grabbing
her bottom. Ms. C said she told her she is never wearing shorts to
school again and commented on how the boys at her school are
disrespectful. Ms. C begins to discuss how this is a rampant issue for
girls and how the administration does nothing about it and/or may
even shame the girls for wearing something that "invites" that kind
of behavior. (excerpt from field notes, 4/3/13)

In this instance, Dalesha decided to leave school because she felt she
had no other recourse to prevent the sexual harassment she was experiencing. Further, as opposed to boys having to change their behavior, it is
Dalesha who decides she will alter her dress for the foreseeable future.

Ebony also discusses the ways she sees the differences between what
boys and girls have to navigate at Jefferson:

Yeah, cuz it's like—the boys . . . it's like it don't really be too much
going on with them but it's like, the girls, it's like, hecka drama,
hecka mess, hecka stuff like that and then it's like when it comes to
the boys and going at towards the girls, it's like the boys disrespect
the girls, tell them stuff, and it's like, you always hear, like, a boy
calling a girl the b word, or a ho, or hecka stuff like that.

Here Ebony notes that girls are faced with more "drama" with one
another, in addition to the regular harassment they face from boys in their
school. In other words, Black girls in her school must navigate both the
"mess" they have with other Black girls and the ways they are consistently
disrespected by Black boys on campus. This precarious positionality illuminates the necessity of Black girls building Black girl solidarity; outside of
the space they have created together, Black girls remain in tension with one
another, and with their male counterparts.

EXCLUSIVELY BLACK SPACES

In recognizing that anti-Blackness is endemic to how we make sense of
human life (Dumas & ross, 2016), exclusively Black spaces in education
are born, created, and in direct response to the rampant anti-Blackness in
the larger world, and in U.S. public schools (ross, in press). Like many of
the MDP students articulated about their Black boy spaces, all students
in this study agreed that there should be more spaces like this for Black

girls. Despite the initial challenges of the space, all students were clear that spaces like these would be a positive force in Black girls' lives. Kenosha notes, "Every school need to have a program like this. Just for us to have a chance. I bet you it'd be so much of a difference, like, it'd be a difference in every school." For Kenosha, the class was not only something that she herself enjoyed; she understands it as a necessary structure in every school serving Black girls. In fact, these spaces are wholly necessary for Black girls to "have a chance." Within Kenosha's statement is a recognition of the myriad obstacles Black girls face in their schools and in life more broadly. Her statement that there would be "so much of a difference" is indicative of what she understands as the current educational Black girl reality.

Ms. C also articulates the magnitude of exclusive spaces themselves. She notes, "I really believe strongly in having our own spaces and I think that it's really important to have a space for folks who identify as such and can just be them . . . I believe in the concept whole-heartedly." A part of "just being them" entails the creation of a space where Black girls can hash out what it means to be themselves in an anti-Black, patriarchal society. Ms. C continues, "So the monoracial space brings up an intensity, but at the same time though, I feel like it has to happen. So I felt like there's some things that girls can get here that they couldn't get in a mixed-race space. There were some things that we would never talk about, ever, even if other people were bringing it up." For Black girls attempting to navigate a school, and a broader society where they may represent the antithesis of an aesthetic norm, openly discussing the aspects of yourself that mark you as unattractive or undesirable can be particularly traumatic. This is especially true for Black girls, as girls and women are more likely to be valued (or not) based on their physical appearance. Yet, in this course, a part of creating Black girl space was the ability to engage in difficult but critical conversations about how we navigate existing as ourselves in hostile environments. Ms. C notes, "All Black girls deserve it. It shouldn't be, like, an extra thing or they get it and then they don't . . . I feel like there was such a high need and I really feel like they deserve it, and I feel like, um, the fact that um the African American Male Achievement is so focused on the males is really missing, they're missing a lot when they do that, with what's happening with Black girls."

Like Moesha, Ms. C is frustrated with a program focused solely on Black boys, as Black girls are consequently erased from the larger conversation on the needs of Black students and denied essential resources and opportunities. As noted earlier, this women's studies class was not (as MDP was) sponsored or supported by a school district. As significant as this space was for the Black girls who participated, it was a "one-off," offered for 1 year as a result of the commitment and dedication of one Black woman instructor. Regardless of the significant ways Black girls experience anti-Blackness in schools, or the overwhelmingly positive impact this exclusively Black-girl space had on everyone involved, at the time the kind of structural support available for Black boys simply didn't exist for Black girls. However, I want to offer that rather than being frustrated with programs that exclusively support Black boys, we might simultaneously celebrate the existence of those programs, while also critiquing any structure that always already presumes the need for this kind of support for Black boys and fails (or refuses) to consider Black girls.

At present, a growing number of initiatives are expanding their missions to include a focus on Black girls and the struggles they face in schools and in society more broadly. One example of this is Oakland Unified School District's new African American Female Excellence Initiative. While this program is still relatively new, the fact that the district has created and is committed to supporting a program specifically for Black girls is a step in the right direction. All of our children deserve institutionalized structural supports that push back against anti-Blackness in schools and in society more broadly. This kind of commitment signals to Black girls that they matter, that their struggles matter, and that their voices will be heard.

NOTES

1. Although a district initiative for Black girls did not exist at the time of this research, Oakland Unified School District recently developed a program for Black girls, African American Female Excellence.

2. I identify geographic region, but use pseudonyms for school names and students so as to protect the confidentiality of the students and educators.

3. #BlackGirlMagic is a hashtag created by CaShawn Thompson to celebrate Black girls and women.

REFERENCES

Adichie, C. (2009). *The danger of a single story* [video file]. Retrieved from www
    .ted.com/talks/chimamanda_adichie_the_danger_of_a_single_story

Brown, A. F. (2011). Descendants of "Ruth": Black girls coping through the "Black
    male crisis." *The Urban Review, 43*(5), 619.

Crenshaw, K., Ocen, P., & Nanda, J. (2015). *Black girls matter: Pushed out, over-
    policed, and underprotected.* New York, NY: African American Policy Forum,
    Center for Intersectionality and Social Policy Studies. Retrieved from www
    .law.columbia.edu/sites/default/files/legacy/files/public_affairs/2015/february
    _2015/black_girls_matter_report_2.4.15.pdf

Dumas, M., & ross, k. m. (2016). "Be real Black for me": Imagining BlackCrit in
    education. *Urban Education, 51*(4), 432.

Givens, J. R., Nasir, N., ross, k., & McKinney de Royston, M. (2016). Modeling manhood: Reimagining Black male identities in school: Modeling manhood. *Anthropology & Education Quarterly, 47*(2), 167–185.

Henderson, N. (2014, June 18). 1,000 women of color want women and girls included in "My Brother's Keeper." *Washington Post.* Retrieved from www .washingtonpost.com/blogs/she-the-people/wp/2014/06/18/1000-women -of-color-want-women-and-girls-included-in-my-brothers-keeper/?utm _term=.468187f70c51

Hurston, Z. N. (2008). *Their eyes were watching God.* New York, NY: Harper. (Original work published 1937.)

Morris, E. W. (2007). "Ladies" or "loudies": Perceptions and experiences of Black girls in classrooms. *Youth & Society, 38*(4), 501.

Nasir, N. S., ross, k. m., McKinney de Royston, M., Givens, J., & Bryant, J. N. (2013). Dirt on my record: Rethinking disciplinary practices in an all-Black, all-male alternative class. *Harvard Educational Review, 83*(3), 489–512.

ross, k. m. (in press). Black space in education: (Anti)blackness in schools and the afterlife of segregation. In Carl A. Grant, Michael J. Dumas, and Ashley N. Woodson (Eds.), *The future is Black: Afropressimism, fugitivity and radical hope in education.* New York, NY: Routledge.

ross, k. m., Nasir, N. S., Givens, J. R., McKinney de Royston, M. M., Vakil, S., Madkins, T. C., & Philoxene, D. (2016). "I do this for all of the reasons America doesn't want me to": The organic pedagogies of Black male instructors. *Equity & Excellence in Education, 49*(1), 85–99.

CHAPTER 10

A View from the Inside

Reflections on the Work

An Interview with Christopher P. Chatmon

In November 2017, Jarvis Givens sat with Christopher Chatmon to get his reflections on the work of the Office of African American Male Achievement, key events and turning points in the journey, and in particular, lessons learned. In this chapter, we present highlights from this insightful interview, organized around several themes that emerged in the conversation.

THE BEGINNING: THE IMPORTANCE OF THE LISTENING TOUR DURING THE FIRST YEAR

The first year was particularly daunting, given the magnitude of the challenge to reverse decades-old achievement patterns and to do so with very little infrastructure, staffing, or specific strategies. Chatmon reflects on the depth of the challenge in the beginning:

It was in 2009 that I was introduced at the school board meeting in September, although there were several conversations prior to that, but formally, this day seven years ago I was introduced as the founding executive director of the African American Male Achievement Initiative, and so there wasn't a blueprint. There wasn't a strategy. We had to imagine a program that did not yet exist. This involved thinking about the set of systems and structures, policies, and practices that would lead to improved educational outcomes for African American male students around literacy, attendance, eliminating the achievement gap, graduation rates, and the reduction of suspension rates.

I was hired as a staff of one. No budget. I actually wasn't even an employee of the district, because of an education code policy, you couldn't have a race-specific initiative, and so I was actually an executive on loan, initially through the East Bay Community Foundation, and then we found a lead fiscal agent, Urban Strategies Council, and I was there for maybe eight months, and then transitioned out of that organization to Partners in School Innovation.

He began working by engaging schools and communities through listening tours.

I think some people laugh when they watch that school board meeting seven years ago where I was introduced. It was awesome, but then people were expecting me to introduce the staff and there were no staff. That first year the focus was on understanding the context. Our superintendent was getting ready to launch a strategic planning process, for which he had 13 different task forces that were looking at different aspects of the ecology of the system. Each task force would produce a report that would inform what would be the next five-year strategic plan. One of those 13 task forces was the African American Male Achievement Taskforce.

We began with a listening tour. And because I couldn't do all of the work myself, we enlisted folks, mostly volunteers, who could help. We talked to Black boys from kindergarten through 12th grade: How are they experiencing school? What did good teaching, good classrooms sound like? How did they describe what a positive school day looked like?

I've got a couple of little flip videos . . . (they don't make flip video cameras anymore) and we just went out to different schools and just had focus groups, led by volunteers (Chantelle Reynolds, Nyeisha DeWitt, Brendon Anderson), with many youth. We used that qualitative data to help tell the story to reframe the issue—it's not Black children, but it's the ecology. It's the ecosystem. That was powerful. More powerful than any research, although we did reference research by Na'ilah Nasir, Pedro Noguera, and Tyrone Howard, among others. We referenced many different folks, different researchers, but for me the most powerful piece in that first month was the listening campaign and the anecdotal, qualitative data. The testimony that came out of that. That really became the impetus of our communication strategy: engage, encourage, and empower.

STARTING WITH THE POSITIVE: THE CONSPIRACY OF CARE

Much has been made, throughout the text, of the twin orientations of love and care in the work of AAMA and MDP. Chatmon underscores the foundational nature of this orientation to the work, and says that it emerged after hearing from Black male youth how negatively they were treated and the lack of care they received in schools:

I began to frame the conversations within the system around this: I wanted people to consciously begin to think about and identify what is a profile of a successful African American child, and what are we doing to create the culture and conditions that lead to all Black children experiencing that success. If you're not thinking about that or talking about that, and all you do is talk about the deficit, all the behavior, then that is what you end up cultivating and perpetuating and priming other people to think that's all they can do.

Every meeting we would go into, we would ask, "How are you engaging Black boys? How are you encouraging Black boys?" I'm going to tell you how powerful this was because 80% of what our kings were telling us, and this was first few weeks of school, first month of school, was that when you see me on my school campus, you don't talk to me. When you see me on my school campus, you engage me as if I've done something wrong or I'm bad or I'm in trouble.

So when teachers and administrators ask, "What's something I can do to support Black boys?" I'd say, know their names. Greet them with a smile. Meet them in hallway. Welcome them to the class with just that . . . Just beginning to get people to think consciously of engaging Black boys, not cowering when you see them . . . Or crossing the street. That's this country's narrative, but we had to shift it, and we were really huge on narrative. Our mayor, Libby Schaaf, quotes me to this day from when she was a city council member and I met with her. She asked me, "Brother Chris, what can I do?" I said, "When you see a young king in your community, one: see him as a king. See him as an asset, and engage him. Encourage him and empower him." Again, not something that's gonna make a tectonic shift, but just calling into your consciousness another way of being.

This shift in consciousness—and in narrative—translated into new practices throughout the district as well.

There are actually some amazing things happening in the school district, but because we're grounded and nested in this negative frame, every conversation we have around Black youth is about everything they're not doing. We never actually look to the collective genius and the amazing things that are happening with Black children every day and Black families. This came to a crescendo early in the work, when a mom reached out to my office. She had contacted her son's principal and said "Hey, my son scored perfect on the STAR test." Kevin. I think Kevin Butler. "And can you guys acknowledge him?" The principal kind of blew her off.

We were doing our community meeting. The next one was at her son's high school. When she called us, you know what I said? "Have him come on up." We're doing our presentation. I'm a call him up to the stage. I had the brothers get him a plaque and a Target gift card and so we gave him a huge community standing ovation. Like, 500 people before we did our breakouts, and somebody asked me, "What about the other African American male students that scored perfect on the state standardized tests?" I said, "You know what? I don't know," so I had our research assessment and data director Jean Wing run the data, and I was like, "Wow, there were 20 African American males that scored perfect on the state standardized test."

And so we did a community day, and I invited all of these kings to get plaques. We acknowledged them. Who picked that up? *Jet* magazine. That was huge on multiple levels. They ran that *Jet* piece. Later I'm listening to a talk show that Cornel West and Tavis Smiley used to have and they say, "We wanna shout out Brother Chris Chatmon. 15 of his kings scored perfect on . . ." It started getting out what we were doing. It was starting to change the narrative of all the negative stuff to actually lifting up some positive things.

THE IMPORTANCE OF PARTNERSHIPS

While care is a clear throughline that makes the transformational work of AAMA possible, it alone is not enough. Building the Office of African American Male Achievement also required institutional and organizational infrastructure, and to do so successfully required partnering with other organizations and institutions, and building from scratch. In some ways, the community engagement process Chatmon discussed above was a key element of his approach to partnership. He modeled that the job of attending to the needs of Black boys in OUSD is the work of the entire district and all of the school communities, but he also engaged in other partnerships that provided political and financial capital.

One example is the partnership with the Office for Civil Rights, whereby a consent decree supported the district in addressing problematic differences in disciplinary actions.

Then a significant shift in the system happened, where the year before, Urban Strategies Council had created a set of reports on the state of African American achievement in the city of Oakland. Those reports made their way up to the United States Department of Education Office for Civil Rights, and then the director of the Office for Civil Rights, who had Oakland roots, Russlyn Ali, looked at those reports.

We incriminated ourselves in the spirit of . . . we acknowledged we were disproportionately suspending Black boys, referring Black boys to special education, and so Russlyn had reached out to Tony, then superintendent, and was like, "Hey, listen. One: you are the first district actually to say, 'You know what? We have a problem, and not only do we have a problem, we actually are gonna do something very different. Have a race-specific strategy, under the auspices of targeted universalism, to really be intentional, unapologetic around looking at this issue, not from the standpoint of fixing Black children, but looking at how do we address the system and the ecology of the public school system.'"

We invited Russlyn in to do a review. Typically, they do a whole compliance review. This was very different. She met with the school board in closed session. We reviewed the reports, and she was enthusiastic about Oakland Unified School District being one of the first districts to partner up with and establish an agreement to resolve a decree.

A consent decree would mean we're in violation and they found this in violation, and they issued a consent decree, where you have to do said things. This was an agreement to resolve disproportionality, and our way to resolve it was having the work embedded in the office of African American Male Achievement. It was at this point that my team and I became employees. People didn't know this. Everyone thought I was a card-carrying member of the Oakland Unified School District. In actuality, I was an employee of another organization.

We went into a resolution agreement with the Office for Civil Rights, which basically says we voluntarily, as a district, will do these different things to address the disproportionate suspension rates of Black boys, as found in violation of Title VI of the Civil Rights Act, and so it was just a key trigger. We're living in very different times now.

Another example is the collaboration with the Obama administration's representative, David Johns, who Chatmon credits with providing the political capital to sustain the work under the first superintendent after Tony Smith. This became important because the subsequent superintendents were not as supportive of AAMA's program.

In the very critical stages, Tony was able to run a level of cover and protectiveness for me while I was building. There were so many haters—from death threats to, "Why Black children? Why Black boys?" Some people were overwhelmingly wanting to see this thing fail. Tony was able, in the two years that he remained, to give me enough runway to lay root and seed, and to build external community partners and begin some strategic activities.

When the new interim superintendent started after Smith, he was not initially a supporter of AAMA. Early on in his tenure, he let me know that at the end of the year my position in the department would be gone. This was a year before My Brother's Keeper, but president 44, Barack Obama, issued an executive order on African American excellence nationally and hired a beautiful, extraordinary young man, by the name of David Johns, who had sent emails to the district for three months, but which no one read. Then finally the communications person for the whole system said, "Hey, Chris. There's this email from this guy David Johns, and no one's really responded. Do you think you could respond to him?" So I looked at the email.

I called David, and I was like, "Listen, bro. I see you are going to be out here next Monday. What do you wanna do?" He was like, "Chris, I wanna lift up you all's work, 'cause I actually think this is a tipping point for other districts to be kind of practicing, modeling what you all are doing," and so he came out for three days, asked me about the pain points, and the opportunities, and we did a listening tour.

We also had a key stakeholder meeting, and the mayor was there. The executive cabinet was there, and key culture keepers in Oakland were there. I had invited the then interim superintendent to come, and he was like, "Oh, I'm double booked, I can't make it," but while we were in the meeting, I truly believe someone texted him and realized that we had someone from the White House.

We issued a media alert. We had ABC, NBC, CBS. We had the *Chronicle*, the *Examiner*. All the local media was there. Well, where was the superintendent? Who knocked on the door to come in the meeting? The superintendent, and at that point, he realized that this was bigger than Oakland. That put our work—still niche, still kind of norming—really on a national platform. That's when overwhelming numbers of people started calling asking to visit and asking what we were doing.

And there were partnerships with foundations in order to build a funding base for the work of the initiative.

Now, we generate about $600,000 in revenue. We have corporate, individual, philanthropic funding. It's all outside. We have outside funding, nested in an open public education fund, and then we've learned how to navigate this system from the entitlements, from local control funding formulas, supplemental and concentrated. It's understanding the funding ecology and not just looking at one stream and trusting it's gonna be there. It's plugging into as many different funding streams, and no one really told me that. I just had to kind of figure that out on my own, and I'm still figuring it out, because in light of where the complete disinvestment is now through president 45, we've got to get more creative now than we've ever been, in terms of sustaining what's still in terms of the infancy of addressing structural racism.

RECRUITMENT AND RETENTION OF TEACHERS

Jerome Gourdine touched on the challenges of recruiting teachers qualified to do the critical work of teaching and leading young people in the Manhood Development Program. Chatmon underscored the nature of these challenges, too, but also how integral the recruitment (and retention) work is to accomplishing the mission of AAMA.

The impetus for the manhood development classes was, "We need Black men in the class. We need Black teachers. Black male teachers." Definitely you need African American male teachers. I think that's core. And we developed the curriculum. We now have seven courses in our African-centered pedagogy. The curriculum focuses on content as well as instructional practice and is centered in principles of brotherhood.

Again, as I've referenced earlier, there is an assault, on not just Black children but Black men; and having a place anywhere in your day, where you actually can close a door and be exactly who you are, and brothers can hold each other, cry, laugh, shout, scream, play, hug, learn, teach, fight, argue. That: we don't have enough of those places. Period. To have that in school, not only has that proven to be powerful for Black children, what we have found even for Black men at my level. Let alone now I have a whole team. By now, we have 24 teachers, but all of us come together twice a month and we close the door. There's no big I's, no little you's. It don't matter what role you play. Brotherhood is the unifying principle, so that is a key and core principle to the manhood development program.

The thing about our work: it wasn't just fifty-thousand-foot-level-focused on policy. That's important, but when people ask me about what is African American Male Achievement, I could take them to schools in Oakland and show them an African American male that we identified and trained, that was working with who? Groups of African American males, and have them interview Black children around their experiences. What that class meant for them in that school, in their life. We identified teachers, that when I first was hired, the school district said, "There's no Black teachers. You can't find Black male teachers." What do we do? We doubled the number of African American male teachers in this district over the course of the last seven years, and our retention rate for a population they said isn't there. We have the highest retention rate: 92% of the African American male teachers that we recruited were retained. Not only are we doing something to identify a population of teachers that they said wasn't there. Our retention rate is higher than the retention rate of the overall system on our first-year, second-year, and third-year teachers, so we're doing something that has implications across the whole system.

CHALLENGES OF THE DISTRICT CONTEXT

While clearly it was at the behest of former superintendent Tony Smith that AAMA was created, and each of the four permanent and interim subsequent superintendents (Gary Yee, Antwan Wilson, Devin Dillon, and Kyla Johnson-Trammell) have all sustained the office and the work, it is no small feat to carry out the race-based work of AAMA in the context of a constantly changing large, urban district.

The constant was me, humbly, but every year, and even multiple times within a year, I have had eight different folks I've reported to. Most of them are gone. I've had the one-to-one meetings with superintendent. I've been on executive cabinet. I've been eliminated from executive cabinet to just a tertiary niche group. I've been in the academic side of the shop. I've been in the community side of the shop. I've been in the office of equity.

I think the long-term game, hopefully, will protect the work; but we moved around from different people. We had Tony Smith. We had Gary Yee. We had Antwan Wilson. We had Devin Dillon, and now we have Kyla Johnson-Trammell; so this is now the fifth superintendent in seven years, and we've been able to not only legitimize the work of African American male achievement in the spirit of this ecosystem. It's also been lifted up as a national best practice.

Another challenge was the changing demographics over the seven years of the initiative.

In October of 2016, we were recognized at the White House as being one of the 25 leading programs that are improving the culture and condition of public schools that lead to improving the educational outcomes for Black boys. That was huge, and so it also gave way to this idea of targeted universalism, as we're looking at data, we notice, wow, you know what? As our demographic is changing, we've lost—since I've been here for seven years—6,800 African American males to now a little under 4,500, and went from 40% of the student population African Americans to now 22%, and Latinos are now 45%. To respond to this, we've given birth to now an Office of Latino Achievement and an Office of Asian Pacific Islander Achievement, and an Office of African American Female Excellence. All of those targeted strategies are nested under the Office of Equity, as a way to support these specific strategies that support children the system has marginalized, but also to inform the system around what are the necessary policy changes, structural changes, that then lead to improved outcomes.

CONCLUDING THOUGHTS

Chatmon concludes the interview with some thoughts about the future, and about how he puts the accomplishments and work of AAMA into perspective.

That's the journey, and now for me it's really legacy work, 'cause I'll just say that the change that I want is not gonna happen in my lifetime. We have manhood development classes in 20-plus schools in Oakland right now. San Francisco Unified went from three schools that are using our curriculum now to seven schools. We have six schools in Seattle, Washington, that have adopted the manhood development class, and I'm gonna be taking 35 kings here on the first week of December to do their first Man Up conference. If you think of where brothers are leaving Oakland, we all going to Pittsburgh and Antioch. Do they know how to deal with our children? Hell no.

It's been this journey of transformation that's definitely accelerated me and then aligning with other folk, so then we could get that out to our students, who actually it's our babies that get it even quicker than our high school students. We're having to deconstruct and reorient who our kings think they are. Moving from one mentality to a king mentality. Because we're not lifting up our history and legacy enough in kindergarten through 12th grade, we have a false sense of who we are, and it gets reinforced in television and corporate culture.

The fact that we actually now have revolutionary literature courses, that we had the Khepera core pathway and academy, that we have our mastering cultural identity, we're doing Man Up conferences, we're training teachers. I'm like, f— talking about it. Just do something.

But We Are Not All The Same!

Unpacking the Layers of Black Male Situations and Circumstances

Tyrone C. Howard

The current status of young Black males presents a complex picture, with much to be said about the manner in which schools, communities, and homes best meet their social, psychological, emotional, cultural, and academic needs. The picture for Black males is promising in some areas, yet distressing in others (Harper & Davis, 2012; Howard, 2016). To that end, it is important to acknowledge that very distinct realities can exist at the same time when discussing the experiences of young Black males. On one hand, multiple data sources provide disturbing accounts of many schools falling woefully short in meeting the needs of Black male students (Allen, 2015). The monolithic picture of doom and gloom often painted, however, is not sufficient to capture the full set of experiences of Black males. An anti-essential framing for Black males is needed. Many Black males are thriving in education, despite schooling conditions that seem to work against their potential, intellect, and promise (Warren, 2013, 2014). This speaks to the resilience, brilliance, and sheer determination that young Black males demonstrate every day in schools. The realities of Black males thriving needs to be highlighted, and these kings must be recognized for their intellectual acumen. This book offers an anti-deficit, anti-essentialist perspective of Black males' performance in schools and gives nuance to the stark realities that young men face—some thriving, some struggling, some making progress, others seeking a place to be recognized for their full human potential. This book also demonstrates how the African American Male Achievement (AAMA) program, with a theory of action dedicated to Targeted Universalism, transformed the system of support for Black males. This book provides us with an approach that seeks to normalize successful outcomes for Oakland Unified School District's lowest-performing subgroup. The realities of Black males are diverse, layered, and complex, and they are represented across the continuum of performance and experience. The work of the African American Male Achievement program recognizes the complexity of Black male identity, and remains steadfastly committed to dramatically improving academic and, ultimately, life outcomes for African American male students in Oakland.

The work highlighted in this book seeks to center the concepts of in-group diversity and complexity in understanding how to better support, teach, care for, and love Black males in ways that this country has often refused to do en masse (Fitzgerald, 2015; Muhammad, 2010). What AAMA has demonstrated to us in this work is that we must move away from the usual, deficit-laden narratives of *"what is wrong with Black males"* and what steps we must take to *"fix Black males."* To the contrary, this work looks to redirect explanations for Black males' experiences and outcomes locally and nationally in a way that recognizes the richness and resilience of their identities, and that, given the appropriate types of support, their promise and potential are bursting at the seams. Home, schools, neighborhoods, churches, mosques, community centers, and everyday locations can all play a role in helping young Black men to realize their full potential academically, socially, emotionally, culturally, and spiritually. The distressing data that I share below suggest that the fixing that is needed is not with Black males but with the structures, policies, practices, curricula, ideologies, teacher attitudes, and programs that exist in schools that Black males negotiate with daily. The African American Male Achievement Initiative offers a remedy and is an example of how loving, caring, and supportive schools for Black males can be established and sustained. Thus, our focus should not be centered on how to *repair* or *remediate Black males*; rather, the suggestion is that these data may lead us to question how we *repair and remediate the interventions, institutions, and (so-called) supports* that seek to serve Black males.

What has been clear for some time is that Black males have lower high school graduation rates, are less likely to be in AP/honors classes, are underrepresented in gifted and talented programs at elementary schools, and typically receive fewer opportunities to learn compared to their White, Asian, and Latino counterparts (Howard, 2008, 2010, 2014). The persistent underperformance is often directly linked to Black males being tracked into remedial or lower-tiered courses at higher rates and having greater likelihood of being in classrooms with underqualified, culturally disconnected teachers and teachers who are likely to have lowered expectations for them.

The work of AAMA is critical because it recognizes how Black males are often perceived and positioned as one of the most problematic groups of students in schools (Ferguson, 2001; Gregory, Skiba, & Noguera, 2010; Milner, McGee, Pabon, & Woodson, 2013). This work operates from a standpoint that the lack of a solid academic foundation in reading, writing, and math skills undoubtedly plays a role in Black males' struggles to thrive in schools, and contributes to many of them being viewed as "problematic" or disciplinary challenges. Without supportive learning communities and cultural understanding from teachers, the likelihood of behavioral challenges increases (Howard, 2008; Noguera, 2003; Skiba, Arredondo, & Williams, 2014; Terriquez, Chlala, & Sacha, 2013). Hence, it is not a stretch to understand that if growing numbers of Black males find themselves in situations where they are victims of educational neglect and underperformance, their behavior becomes more of a challenge, which subsequently contributes to larger numbers of students who are ultimately "pushed out," suspended, or ultimately expelled from schools. A recent report by Wood, Harris, and Howard (2018) found the following:

- In the state of California, which has the fifth-largest Black population in the nation, the statewide suspension rate for Black males is 3.6 times higher than the statewide rate for all students. Specifically, while 3.6% of all students were suspended in 2016-2017, the suspension rate for Black boys and young men was 12.8%.
- The highest suspension disparity by grade level occurs in early childhood education (grades K through 3), where Black boys are 5.6 times more likely to be suspended than the state average.
- Black male students who are classified as "foster youth" are suspended at noticeably high rates, at 27.4%. Across all analyses, Black males who were foster youth in 7th and 8th grade represented the subgroup that had the highest percentage of Black male suspensions, at 31.0%.

THE CHALLENGE AND THE RESPONSE

The information in this work is vital because the authors highlight the extensive data that show that Black children (and boys in particular) face a myriad of challenges before entering school, which requires further analysis. Issue such as higher infant mortality rates than Whites (Murphy, Xu, & Kochanek, 2012; Wilson, 2008), greater likelihood of being born into poverty, and having less access to adequate health care compared to White, Asian, and Latino children requires transdisciplinary intervention (Brookings Institute, 2011; U.S. Department of Commerce, 2009). It is important to note some of these realities, because what they reflect are serious challenges that exist in many communities where Black males may reside and speak to larger social-structural challenges. Wilson (2008) uncovers many of these realities, making a sociological analysis of how and why institutions and public and social policy have fallen short in providing Black people, and Black males in particular, a realistic chance for educational and life success. Hence, structural inequities and challenges confront Black males early, often, and more persistently than they do many, if not most, of their peers. Some have gone further by stating that the state of affairs for Black males is more of a public health issue than previous research has suggested (Hilfiker, 2002).

AN EXPANDED PICTURE

In light of the dismal data on Black males, it is important to share a more complete and positive narrative. Howard and colleagues (2016) in their counternarrative study documented the plights of high-achieving Black and Latino males and identified young men who were thriving in their homes, neighborhoods, and schools in ways that are often not reported in the professional literature. Harper and colleagues (2014) engaged in similar work documenting the "succeeding in the city" of high school–age Black and Latino males in New York City. These accounts are needed to provide examples to school districts across the nation that Black male success is possible, and that it is happening in cities and schools. It is important to note that after decades of seeing youth incarceration rise, the number of youth who are incarcerated has declined notably over the past 10 years, which has had important implications for Black boys, who are typically overrepresented in jails and prisons. More recently a report from Wilcox, Wang, and Mincy (2018) revealed how Black men are doing better in many ways, and how larger numbers of them are now part of a growing middle class, finding economic mobility, and recognizing fiscal realities that were not always present. The report states:

> much of the racial news and academic research on black men in America has been sobering, if not downright depressing. But negative news isn't the only story about race or even about black males in the United States. In *Black Men Making It in America*, we report some good news:
>
> • **Black men's economic standing.** More than one-in-two black men (57%) have made it into the middle class or higher as adults today, up from 38% in 1960, according to a new analysis of Census data. And the share of black men who are poor has fallen from 41% in 1960 to 18% in 2016. So, a substantial share of black men in America are realizing the American Dream—at least financially—and a clear majority are not poor.

- **The institutional engines of black men's success.** As expected, higher education and full-time work look like engines of success for black men in America. But three other institutions that tend to get less attention in our current discussions of race—the U.S. military, the black church, and marriage—also appear to play significant roles in black men's success. . . .
- **The importance of individual agency.** Black men who score above average in their sense of agency—measured by reports that they feel like they are determining the course of their own lives versus feeling like they do not have control over the direction of their lives—as young men or teenagers in the late 1970s are more likely to be prosperous later in life. (Wilcox, Wang, & Mincy, 2018, p. 3)

One of the problems with the current literature on Black males is an almost exclusive focus on them as being poor and residing in urban communities, and the challenges that are present in such environments. Many of the challenges that confront Black males in education go beyond their communities and their social-class status and are directly located in classrooms, including the lack of racial awareness and cultural ignorance among school personnel, apathetic teacher attitudes, and poor-quality instruction that they receive, be it in urban, rural, or suburban schools (Mincy, 2006, 2007; Howard, 2008). The monolithic portrayal of Black males in poor urban communities fails to consider the increasing social-class diversity among Black males. Gordon (2012) asserts that approximately one-third of Black families live in suburban communities and send their children to middle-class schools where they still underperform compared to their White peers. Thus, even the so-called privileges that accompany social and economic mobility do not seem to thwart the presence of race and racism when it comes to the schooling experiences of Black males. Harper and Nichols (2008) make the claim that there is a need to examine the unique and diverse experiences of Black males and to develop an understanding of various subgroups.

When discussing Black males, we must be willing to ask: to which Black males are we referring (Harper & Associates, 2014)? While there are many common experiences across the Black male spectrum, there is a need to examine the experiences of middle-class and affluent Black males, as well as those who identify as LGBTQ, in addition to those Black males from mixed-race backgrounds and those individuals with disabilities. There is also a pressing need to examine the experiences of the growing numbers of Black males experiencing homelessness, those in foster care, those dealing with mental health issues, and even young men who are teen fathers and relative caregivers.

To be clear, it is salient to give attention to in-group diversity. The need to challenge the monolithic account of Black males is long overdue.

Amechi and colleagues (2016) contend that "the proclivity for treating all Black men as the same often leads to one-size-fits-all programmatic interventions" (p. 102). Therefore, understanding the challenges of race, gender, positionality, and other social identities for Black males is crucial to any thorough examination of their schooling experiences. The intersectionality of race, class, and gender and other identity markers is fundamentally critical in research concerned with young Black males, as they are in the case of any subgroup (Crenshaw, 1989, 1995). Each marker in its own way profoundly influences identity construction, self-concept, interactions with the world, and meaning-making. Again, Black males possess multiple identities that are profoundly shaped by race, socioeconomic status, and gender in all of their complex manifestations. Needless to say, the picture of Black boys and men is conflicting; while some progress is seen for some of them, far too many still suffer from the pernicious effects of structural inequities, racism, criminalization, poverty, and deficit constructions of their promise and potential. To that end, educational practitioners, researchers, policymakers, and advocates must remain steadfast in efforts to remove barriers that restrict the ability of Black males to be whole, healthy, and human. Within the educational context of moving work on Black boys forward, and being cognizant of the important work that AAMA is doing in Oakland, the following recommendations are offered as critical starting points in this important work.

Recognize that cultural differences are not cultural deficits. One of the biggest strengths of AAMA is to build on culture as a strength. A factor that may explain the large numbers of suspensions and expulsions of Black males from schools is the general cultural disconnect that occurs between many teachers and students. In particular, culture influences cognition, thinking, speaking, behavior, and learning. Many Black boys frequently find themselves in classrooms with teachers who have limited to no understanding of their cultural ways of knowing, thinking, communicating, and being. A more nuanced and deeper understanding of culture recognizes the complexities of day-to-day behaviors, context, history, and practices that are germane for all learners. But for Black males, their ways of expression, processing new information, and caring are often misunderstood and deemed to be problematic. AAMA's focus on decreasing suspensions and expulsions by honoring and celebrating culture is vital to connectedness and learning. School staff must recognize that cultural differences among students do not mean cultural deficits. However, districts must not adopt static notions of culture either, but recognize the variability of Black culture and Black male students and help teachers develop culturally appropriate practices, culturally inclusive content, and learning environments that recognize and honor cultural democracies.

Intensive, ongoing, professional development. Black boys and young men are more likely to be viewed as deviant or troublemakers, even at the earliest of ages. This is due to wider societal stereotypes and depictions of Black males that present them as criminalized, pathological, or troublesome in the media. AAMA's success with putting Black men in positions to model how to mentor, support, care for, and teach Black boys can serve as model for schools across the nation. To that end, schools across the board can benefit from intensive, ongoing professional development that should be provided to all educators (e.g., staff, teachers, administrators, counselors) on topics such as unconscious bias, racial microaggressions, culturally mediated behaviors, and teaching practices for boys and young men of color. Professional development provided by experts on Black boys should be designed to raise educators' awareness about these issues and build their capacities by exposing them to concrete alternative strategies such as classroom management and relationship-building with students.

Understand the multiple layers of male identity. The significance of identity for Black youth has been discussed in previous research (Nasir, 2012). This work has important implications for Black males, and needs to be further elaborated. In Flennaugh's (2016) work, for example, he discussed how identity for Black males is highly nuanced, dynamic, complicated, and increasingly complex. Therefore, it is vital that researchers and practitioners engage in more robust examinations and understanding of identity and self-concept. Self-concept is made up of many selves—different worlds that are constructed in such a way that some worlds may be more significant in an individual's self-concept.

Teacher-student relationships beyond the classroom. School administrators, teachers, and staff should make the effort to learn about the lives, interests, and homes of these young men and the cultural wealth they hold in order to understand students beyond the classroom. Many of the staff in AAMA make personal connections with the kings, learning about their home lives, querying them about their life dreams and aspirations, and taking an interest in them that goes beyond academics. While teachers have lessons to plan, assignments to grade, and lives of their own, many Black males (like other students) speak highly of the teachers and staff who care about them, invest in them, empathize with them, get to know them, go the extra mile to support them academically and socially/emotionally, inquire about their personal lives, and even take on mentoring roles in their lives. Schools serve as a second home for many of our students, and as such, school administrators, teachers, and staff should be intentional in developing a culture of care, concern, and commitment to young men academically, socially, and emotionally.

School and community organizations: providing social and emotional support. Students that are exposed to diverse organizations, including community-based organizations at their school sites that meet many of their needs, can do notably better than their peers who are not exposed to such organizations. By incorporating a revolutionary literature course that is centered in history, culture, and community, AAMA students are exposed to local organizations, historical figures, and movements that are germane to the struggle for racial, economic, and social justice in their own neighborhoods. Organizations that are the most influential typically provide multidimensional support that keeps students engaged in school, sustains and enhances their interest in academics, and alleviates stress for students. School organizations and community-based organizations should work in concert to consider ways to provide students holistic support.

Assessment of discipline policies and practices. To be clear, Black students are harmed most by punitive policies and practices in schools nationwide. The alarming levels of racial disproportionality in school discipline have been well documented (Nasir, ross, McKinney de Royston, Givens, & Bryant, 2013; Wood, Harris, & Howard, 2018). Schools can take important steps to address school policies and discipline in multiple ways. AAMA has established as one of its primary goals the reduction of school- and district-level suspensions and expulsions. Such explicit goals should be part of what schools take up nationally. An initial start can be the elimination of suspension in early childhood education (Wood, Essien, & Blevins, 2017). A second step can be to establish measurable targets to reduce suspensions and expulsions across schools and districts, and to engage in ongoing evaluations of the school sites, grade levels, and even specific classrooms where the levels of Black male referrals and suspensions are highest. A third step can be the establishment of district-wide task forces to study discipline practices across the board to identify both schools where problems seem to be prevalent and sites where racial disproportionality in school discipline is nonexistent. A consistent and intense focus that is centered less on punishment and exclusion and more on restorative discipline and support can go a long way in helping to keep Black males in schools, engaged, and focused on learning.

REFERENCES

Alexander, M. (2010). *The new Jim Crow.* New York, NY: The New Press.
Allen, Q. (2015). Race, culture and agency: Examining the ideologies and practices of U.S. teachers of Black male students. *Teaching and Teacher Education 47,* 71–81.

Amechi, M. H., Berhanu, J., Cox, J. M., McGuire, K. M., Morgan, D. L., Williams, C. D., & Williams, M. S. (2016). Understanding the unique needs and experiences of Black male subgroups at four-year colleges and universities. In S. R. Harper & L. Wood (Eds.), *Advancing Black male student success from preschool through Ph.D.* (pp. 101–124). Sterling, VA: Stylus Publishers.

Brookings Institute. (2011). *The recession's ongoing impact on America's children: Indicators of children's economic well-being through 2011.* Retrieved from brookings.edu/research/papers/2011/12/20-children well-being-isaacs

Crenshaw, K. (1989) Demarginalizing the intersection of race and sex: A Black feminist critique of antidiscrimination doctrine, feminist theory and antiracist politics. *University of Chicago Legal Forum, 1989,* p. 139–167.

Crenshaw, K. (1995). Mapping the margins: Intersectionality, identity politics, and violence against women of color. In K. Crenshaw, N. Gotanda, G. Pellet, & K. Thomas (Eds.), *Critical race theory: The key writings that formed the movement* (pp. 357–383). New York, NY: The New Press.

Ferguson, A. A. (2001). *Bad boys: Public schools in the making of Black masculinity* (Reprint ed.). Ann Arbor, MI: University of Michigan Press.

Fitzgerald, T. D. (2015). *Black males and racism: Improving the schooling and life chances of African Americans.* New York, NY: Routledge.

Flennaugh, T. K. (2016). Mapping me: Mapping identity among academically high-performing Black males. *Teachers College Record, 118*(6). Retrieved from www.tcrecord.org/library/content.asp?contentid=19962

Gordon, B. (2012). "Give a brotha a break!": The experiences and dilemmas of middle-class African American male students in white suburban schools. *Teachers College Record, 114*(5), 1–13.

Gregory, A., Skiba, R. J., & Noguera, P. A. (2010). The achievement gap and the discipline gap: Two sides of the same coin? *Educational Researcher, 39*(1), 59–68.

Harper, S. R., & Associates. (2014). *Succeeding in the city: A report from the New York City Black and Latino male high school achievement study.* Philadelphia, PA: University of Pennsylvania, Center for Study of Race and Equity in Education.

Harper, S. R., & Davis, C. H. F., III. (2012). They (don't) care about education: A counternarrative of Black male students' responses to inequitable schooling. *Educational Foundations, 26*(1/2), 103–120.

Harper, S. R., & Nichols, A. H. (2008). Are they not all the same? Racial heterogeneity among Black male undergraduates. *Journal of College Student Development, 49*(3), 199–214.

Hilfiker, D. (2002). *Urban injustice. How ghettoes happen.* New York, NY: Seven Stories Press.

Howard, T. C. (2008). Who really cares? The disenfranchisement of African American males in prek-12 schools: A critical race theory perspective. *Teachers College Record, 110,* 954–985.

Howard, T. C. (2014). *Black male(d): Peril and promise in the education of African American males.* New York, NY: Teachers College Press.

Howard, T. C., & Associates (2017). *The counter narrative: Reframing success of high achieving Black and Latino males in Los Angeles County.* Los Angeles: University of California, Los Angeles, UCLA Black Male Institute.

Milner, H. R. (2007). African American males in urban schools: No excuses—teach and empower. *Theory into Practice 46*(3), 239–246.

Milner, H. R., IV, McGee, E., Pabon, A., & Woodson, A. (2013). Teacher education and Black male students in the United States of America. *Multidisciplinary Journal of Educational Research, 3*(3), 235–263.

Mincy, R. B. (2006). *Black males left behind*. Washington, DC: The Urban Institute.

Muhammad, K. G. (2010). *The condemnation of Blackness: Race, crime, and the making of modern urban America.* Cambridge, MA: Harvard University Press.

Murphy, S. L., Xu, J. Q., & Kochanek, K. D. (2012). Deaths: Preliminary data for 2010. *National Vital Statistics Reports, 60*(4).

Nasir, N. (2012). *Racialized identities: Race and achievement for African-American youth.* Stanford, CA: Stanford University Press.

Nasir, N., ross, k., McKinney de Royston, M., Givens, J., & Bryant, J. (2013). Dirt on my record: Rethinking disciplinary practices in an all-Black, all-male alternative class. *Harvard Educational Review, 83*(3), 489–512.

National Center for Education Statistics (2016). *Trends in high school dropout and completion rates in the United States.* Retrieved from nces.ed.gov/programs/dropout/ind_01.asp

Noguera, P. A. (2003). The trouble with Black boys: The role and influence of environmental and cultural factors on the academic performance of African American males. *Urban Education, 38,* 431–459.

Skiba, R. J., Arredondo, M. I., & Williams, N. T. (2014). More than a metaphor: The contribution of exclusionary discipline to a school-to-prison pipeline. *Equity & Excellence in Education, 47,* 546–564.

Terriquez, V., Chlala, R., & Sacha, J. (2013). *The impact of punitive high school discipline policies on the postsecondary trajectories of young men* (Research brief). Los Angeles, CA: Pathways to Postsecondary Success.

Warren, C. A. (2013). The utility of empathy for White female teachers' culturally responsive interactions with Black male students. *Interdisciplinary Journal of Teaching and Learning, 3*(3), 175–200.

Warren, C. A. (2014). Towards a pedagogy for the application of empathy in culturally diverse classrooms. *The Urban Review, 46*(3), 395–419.

Wilcox, W. B., Wang, W. R., & Mincy, R. B. (2018). Black men making it in America: The engines of economic success for Black men in America. American Enterprise Institute. Retrieved from www.aei.org/wp-content/uploads/2018/06/BlackMenMakingItInAmerica-Final_062218.pdf

Wilson, W. J. (2008). *More than just race: Being Black and poor in the inner city.* New York, NY: Norton & Simon.

Wood, J. L., Essien, I., & Blevins, D. (2017). Black males in kindergarten: The effect of social skills on close and conflictual relationships with teachers. *Journal of African American Males in Education, 8*(2), 30–50.

Wood, J. L., Harris, F., III, & Howard, T. C. (2018). *Get out! Black Male suspensions in California public schools.* San Diego, CA: Community College Equity Assessment Lab and the UCLA Black Male Institute.

Lessons from the Town

Implementing a New Approach to the Education of African American Male Students in Oakland

Pedro A. Noguera

When Chris Chatmon, the founding director of the African American Male Achievement (AAMA) Initiative in Oakland, first told me in 2010 about the work he was planning to undertake with African American males, I was skeptical. My skepticism was not based on any doubts about Chris Chatmon. I had known him for years, and his track record as a dedicated leader in youth development work, particularly in his former role as the executive director of the East Oakland Youth Development Center, left me with no doubt that there was no one better to lead such an initiative. My skepticism came from my knowledge of the Oakland public schools and the daunting challenges he would face working there. I knew the Oakland Unified School District well. I taught in several schools throughout the district shortly after moving to the Bay Area in 1981. Over a 20-year period I worked closely with the various superintendents and school board members who have led the district. My past experience left me skeptical and with very little confidence that the school district could do anything helpful to support Black boys. I feared that Chatmon was being set up to fail.

Despite my reservations, we talked at length about what could be accomplished through the new office he had been charged to create, and the obstacles he was likely to encounter when working in Oakland schools. I was intimately familiar with the obstacles facing schools in Oakland. In addition to my teaching experience in the district, from 1990–1993 I worked closely with Lowell Middle School in West Oakland, one of the poorest neighborhoods in the city (City of Oakland, 1994). I partnered with Dr. Rosalyn Upshaw, the principal, and Afriye Quamina (aka "Brother Q"), in a project supported by the University of California Office of the President that aimed to bring research-based supports and interventions to the school and its students (Noguera, 1996). From my experience at Lowell over those three years, I learned that the district was clueless about how to support its efforts to improve, and I saw that without adequate resources it was extremely difficult to disrupt the cycle of failure that the school was mired in, despite the best efforts of many dedicated educators and community activists.

In 1995, I was invited to serve on a task force created by former Superintendent Dr. Carolyn Getridge. The task force was charged with addressing the pervasive underachievement (the average GPA for Black high school students at the time was 1.6) and high rates of suspensions and expulsions of African American students. These patterns were evident throughout most schools in the district and the schools wanted expert advice on how to address the problem. I agreed to serve because I appreciated the magnitude of what was clearly a crisis. But even then I was hesitant. I had seen similar initiatives undertaken in Oakland before.[1] I doubted that the task force would be allowed to ask tough questions about the efficacy of key personnel, that we would be provided with access to the data needed to assess the quality of schools and district programs. I doubted that we'd be given permission to investigate how money was being spent. Without such a purview I didn't think it would be possible to address the full extent of the challenges preventing most schools in Oakland from meeting the needs of African American students. Given that Black students were the majority in the district and that the city (at the time) was predominantly Black, I understood why the district leadership felt pressure to figure out how to address such a glaring failure. After all, this was Oakland, the community that had given birth to the Black Panther Party, the community that had seen its first Black superintendent, Marcus Foster, assassinated. Furthermore, the current superintendent, a majority of the school board, and most senior administrators in the district were Black (as were the mayor, the majority on the city council, the city manager, police chief, and congressman). Surely, there should be enough wisdom, experience, and commitment among them to ensure that Black children were being well served by the public schools. Nonetheless, I had my doubts.

At the time I was a new, overcommitted, and untenured professor of education at UC Berkeley. I had just completed a 4-year term as an elected member of the Berkeley School Board and I wanted to devote my time to scholarship and research that I believed would support efforts to address the complexities of racial inequality in education. Despite my misgivings about the district, I agreed to serve because I hoped that the task force would confront the institutional challenges facing the district that contributed to the high rates of failure among Black students, and I was willing to help the leadership devise solutions to the chronic problems it faced.

After our first meeting, I realized that my initial skepticism was warranted. Members of the task force were provided with an overview of the major programs in the district starting with the early childhood program.

We were provided with a brief description of what was offered to children and families, and given data on the population served. The presentation was to be followed by another on elementary schools in the district. But before moving to the next report, I insisted on posing some questions to the administrator. I asked: "Would you characterize any of these programs as 'high quality'?" During my years of teaching in Oakland I had seen many of the early childhood programs in various parts of the city. Based on my observations I had quickly come to the conclusion that rather than offering the type of high-quality early childhood education that research shows is essential for providing children with an educational foundation for learning, these programs offered little more than babysitting. The ones I had visited were staffed by untrained teachers, and the facilities were not well maintained. The administrator was caught off guard. Her response was that the programs were in compliance with state and federal guidelines. I then asked if she or any of the members of the task force would put our own children in these programs. Again, she was caught off guard and muttered, "That's really up to you." I responded that if the programs were not good enough for members of the task force to enroll their own children, we should acknowledge that they were inadequate and should be overhauled.

My suggestion was "noted" by the task force chair, and we were instructed to continue our review of district programs. That was the last meeting I attended. I knew then that the serious inquiry I had hoped would be part of our work would not occur. However, to my surprise, a few weeks after I had stopped attending the meetings the task force became embroiled in controversy and became the subject of national media attention, much of it derisive. After I left, members of the task force had developed a recommendation calling for Ebonics to be recognized as an official second language, since it was spoken by many African American students. The recommendation was supported by my colleague John Ogbu, the highly respected anthropologist at UC Berkeley. He and several others contended that Ebonics should be treated as a distinct language, rather than as a dialect of "bad English," and the task force called for children who spoke Ebonics to be provided with additional educational support, similar to that provided to children who were non-English speakers.[2]

Despite the fact that the Ebonics resolution had been supported by a number of prominent scholars and research associations (Dillard, 1973), the media and several policymakers belittled and castigated the Oakland public schools for the Ebonics resolution. The intent of the recommendation, which I, too, supported, was never covered by the media. Instead, Oakland was lambasted for calling for Black children to learn Ebonics, which was a deliberate misinterpretation of the recommendation. Meanwhile, the larger purpose behind the creation of the task force—to devise strategies to improve the academic performance of African American students—was forgotten. No critical review of district schools or programs was undertaken, and once the media frenzy subsided, it became clear that there would be no substantive change in the approach taken to educate African American children for some time.

More than 20 years after the task force on African American Achievement concluded its work, Chatmon was appointed to head the office of African American Male Achievement (AAMA) by a new superintendent, Dr. Tony Smith. I knew Tony because he had been a doctoral student at UC Berkeley. I met with him shortly after his appointment and was struck by his commitment to making a difference for the children of Oakland. Though we never discussed the details of his plan to create AAMA, I tried to warn him, based on my past experience, that he might be being set up to fail. I believed that unless principals across the district were required to work with him, and unless he was provided with adequate resources to support African American males in the district, he would not be able to improve academic outcomes for this population of students.

Fortunately, Chatmon and the AAMA have proven me wrong. While there has not been an overall improvement for African American male students in Oakland, AAMA has shown that with the right combination of mentorship, counseling, academic enrichment, and support, significant gains can be obtained. Wisely, Chatmon scaled back the scope and goals of the AAMA such that it did not focus on serving all African American males in the district. Instead, it provides the type of targeted support to a select number of schools and students that research shows is most effective (Garibaldi, 1992). The evidence shows that those who receive the interventions—mentorship, a special class focused on manhood development, and counseling—have experienced significant improvements in attendance, a reduction in discipline referrals, and an overall increase in academic performance (Watson, 2014). In short, Chatmon and his small staff have accomplished what neither the task force I served on, nor a series of superintendents appointed since then, have been able to.

AAMA is particularly good at helping young men deal with what Edyson Julio (2018) has described as PTS—Performance to Survive. Julio, like Majors and Bilson (1993) before, describes the dilemma that many Black males contend with as they strive to improve their lives and pursue their education while simultaneously maintaining credibility on the streets. In an article for *Harvard Education Magazine* he writes:

> In all of my time as an educator working with justice-involved youth and teaching in prisons or public high schools, I've never met a single student who could shake off the limitations of urban culture. This culture demands of us a performance—a way of existing in the world that ensures our bodily safety

first, but makes us prone to behaviors that undermine our learning. I see it in the exaggerated maleness, or the spurning of education. I see it in the anger directed at students who are smart, or the ways violence is celebrated in the classroom. None of these behaviors make for a strong student. But for the urban student, actions that seem unruly to educators are effective—indeed necessary—ways of surviving. Accordingly then, I have termed this condition PTS: Performing to Survive. It is one I suspect a mass of black and Latinx folks living in the urban space experience, myself included. (Julio, 2018)

AAMA has found a way to address PTS so that the Black male students it serves are equipped with the academic skills to excel in the classroom and the social skills to navigate the challenges on the streets. Several of the chapters in this volume elaborate further on these strategies. For educators, policymakers, community advocates, and others who seek to address the educational needs of African American males, this could be invaluable advice. There are many districts across America faced with similar challenges. More often than not, the problems that disproportionately beset African American male children—special education placements in restrictive settings, punitive discipline referrals, underperformance in core academic subjects—are simply accepted as "normal." The chapters in this book offer insights into what can be done to address the pervasive problem of Black male underachievement and to disrupt the dismal status quo. Furthermore, if reading isn't sufficient, site visits to Oakland can be arranged so that even doubters who deep down inside believe that students who are written off as uneducable, unreachable, and incorrigible cannot be helped, can see with their own eyes that such children can be served well, and that better results can be obtained.

Yet, even as we share the findings from evaluations of AAMA and make visible the lessons learned from 8 years of relentless work and commitment, it is likely that the lessons will not be applied elsewhere even though the issues facing Black male students in Oakland are common to many communities throughout the United States. Despite the fact that the consequences of continued failure are so costly, in human and financial terms, I fear that most school districts will not take on the challenge of creating and implementing a program like this, mostly because they lack the will and resolve to pull all of the essential ingredients together that make this work possible. These ingredients include strong, visionary leadership; community and parental support; and institutional support (especially funding) that extends beyond the commitments of a single superintendent. Anyone who has followed the travails of school reform in America over the last 20 years knows that while the problems remain, particularly in communities like Oakland where poverty is concentrated, policy is more likely to focus on reforms like expanding the number of charter schools;

using phonics to teach reading; creating new, small schools; expanding access to technology; high-stakes testing; and so on. Strategies that evidence shows are working to improve outcomes for underserved populations are often less likely to be embraced than the latest fad or "innovations," even though these reforms often amount to little more than a gimmick and an unfulfilled promise.

There have been many unfulfilled promises in Oakland. The same is true in other cities where I have worked, such as Newark, Baltimore, Detroit, and Washington, D.C. In large swaths of Black communities in these cities, there is anger and bitterness over promises that have not been kept. New superintendents have been appointed who have issued sweeping promises while ushering in new reforms. Few have stayed for more than 3 years, barely enough time to see their reforms through. The strength of AAMA is its consistency, the ability of its leaders to adapt to the needs of Black male students and their families, and the ability of the staff to learn and to improve the interventions offered over time.

Nearly 100 years ago, the noted African American scholar W. E. B. Du Bois wrote at length about a concept he referred to as "double consciousness." He described this as "a peculiar sensation," of "always looking at one's self through the eyes of others." He writes,

> One ever feels his two-ness, an American, a Negro; two souls, two thoughts, two unreconciled strivings; two warring ideals in one dark body, whose dogged strength alone keeps it from being torn asunder . . . He simply wishes to make it possible for a man to be both a Negro and an American without being cursed and spit upon by his fellows, without having the doors of opportunity closed roughly in his face. (Sundquist, 1996, p. 102)

The double consciousness described by Du Bois is still very present today. It is as evident in the slogan "Black Lives Matter" as it was in its precursors, "I am Somebody" and "I am a Man." Such assertions are a pointed reminder that we are not equal. As long as Black lives are being taken repeatedly by the police, in public and on camera, and police officers are exonerated for the murders, then we know that our assertions that we matter, that we are somebody, and that we are men (or women), resonate only with some. Our double consciousness is evident when we witness so much public anguish and sympathy for the White opioid crisis while we know that no help was offered to ease the suffering in Black communities in the 1980s when we were in the midst of the crisis created by the pervasive availability of crack cocaine. Clearly, we have not yet arrived at a stage where all lives matter, and where all children are regarded as worthy of fair treatment and equal opportunity.

This is why the work of the African American Male Achievement Initiative is so important. History has shown that there are very few cases where Black communities can count on public schools to improve educational outcomes and opportunities for Black children. Without targeted interventions undertaken by knowledgeable and committed educators who understand the importance of partnering with parents and the community, it is not possible to bring about positive change.

To bring about change on a larger scale it will undoubtedly be necessary for the educational needs of African American boys and girls to be regarded as an "American problem," rather than a "Black problem." Perhaps if this were the case there would be an urgent response to their needs, one that channels the necessary resources to schools overwhelmed by poverty and trauma. In order for districts like Oakland to become successful, they must become truly invested in improving outcomes for Black males and other underserved populations, and they must be provided with sufficient support so that every school is equipped with the resources necessary to meet the needs of these students.

We are not there yet, in Oakland or in most other communities in the United States. For that reason there is a dire need for programs like AAMA and the leaders behind it. Ideally, the work being done by Chatmon and his colleagues at AAMA should be the work undertaken by every superintendent and principal who has agreed to assume a role of educational leadership at schools and districts serving Black children.

For now, this is wishful thinking. But we should not stop aspiring to the possibility that we can in fact alter the outcomes and improve the lives of Black boys and girls through quality education.

NOTES

1. For a discussion of past initiatives see Commission for Positive Change in the Oakland Public Schools (1990).

2. For a full discussion of the controversy created by the Ebonics resolution, see Perry and Delpit (1997).

REFERENCES

City of Oakland. (1994). *West Oakland community—Existing conditions*. Oakland, CA: Office of Economic Development.

Commission for Positive Change in the Oakland Public Schools. (1990). *Good education in Oakland: Strategies for positive change*. Oakland, CA: Author.

Dillard, J. (1972). *Black English*. New York, NY: Vintage Books.

Garibaldi, A. (1992). Educating and motivating African American males to succeed. *Journal of Negro Education*, 61(1), 4–11.

Julio, E. (2018, Summer). Creating another self to survive. *Harvard Education Magazine*. Retrieved from www.gse.harvard.edu/news/ed/18/05/creating-another-self-survive

Majors, R., & Billson, M. (1993). *Cool pose: The dilemmas of Black manhood in America*. New York, NY: Simon and Schuster.

Noguera, P. (1996). Confronting the urban in urban school reform. *Urban Review*, 28(1), 1–19.

Perry, T., & Delpit, L. (1997). The real Ebonics debate. *Rethinking Schools*, 12(1).

Sundquist, E. J. (1996). *The Oxford W. E. B. Du Bois reader*. New York, NY: Oxford University Press.

Watson, V. (2014, December). *The Black Sonrise: Oakland Unified School District's commitment to address and eliminate institutional racism*. An evaluation report prepared for the Office of African American Male Achievement. Oakland, CA: Oakland Unified School District. Retrieved from www.ousd.org/cms/lib07/CA01001176/Centricity/Domain/78/TheBlackSonrise_WebV2_sec.pdf

About the Contributors

Baayan Bakari has been an educator within the Oakland community for more than 20 years. He is currently an educational consultant with the Oakland Unified School District's Office of African American Male Achievement. He has written more than seven University of California–approved courses and provided curriculum and professional development for facilitators within the district. He was a classroom teacher for six years at a school in the heart of East Oakland. In 1996 he won an Echoing Green Fellowship to begin the Amafula Manhood Training curriculum, which later developed into the Khepera Curriculum. Baayan was the national director of training for the Mentoring Center in Oakland, CA, where he was a member of the executive team and managed federal, state, and local budgets. Baayan has also managed several community-based programs, including Oakland Freedom Schools, an initiative of Marian Wright Edelman's Children's Defense Fund and has received numerous honors for his creative approaches to community and youth development, including a prestigious award from the Echoing Green Foundation. In 2010, Baayan was selected by Susan L. Taylor (former editor-in-chief of *Essence* magazine) to serve on a national committee to design a national infrastructure that reintegrates former inmates into society.

Christopher P. Chatmon serves as deputy chief of equity for the Oakland Unified School District (OUSD) and was named as a "Leader to Learn From" by *Education Week* magazine. Chatmon was selected as a Campaign for Black Male Achievement "Social Innovation Accelerator," because he is committed to improving life outcomes for all youth and especially for African American males. He is founding executive director of OUSD's Office of African American Male Achievement, was principal of an alternative high school in San Francisco, and served as executive director of urban services at the YMCA in Oakland for more than 10 years. Chatmon earned an MA in education and a secondary teaching credential in social science from Brown University. He also holds a BS in psychology with a minor in physical education from San Francisco State University.

Shawn Ginwright is a leading national expert on African American youth, youth activism, and youth development. He is an associate professor of education in the Africana Studies Department and senior research associate for the Cesar E. Chavez Institute for Public Policy at San Francisco State University. His research examines the ways in which youth in urban communities navigate through the constraints of poverty and struggle to create equality and justice in their schools and communities. In 1989, Dr. Ginwright founded Leadership Excellence Inc., an innovative youth development agency located in Oakland, CA, that trains African American youth to address pressing social and community problems. In 2002 he also created the Research Collaborative on Youth Activism, a network of scholar activists who study, advocate for, and support youth organizing efforts around the country. Dr. Ginwright currently serves on the board of directors for the California Endowment, with oversight of a 3-billion-dollar endowment to improve the health of California's underserved communities.

Jarvis R. Givens is an assistant professor at the Harvard Graduate School of Education (HGSE) and the Suzanne Young Murray Assistant Professor at the Radcliffe Institute, having earned his PhD in African diaspora studies from the University of California, Berkeley. Givens's research falls at the intersection of the history of American education, 19th- and 20th-century African American history, and critical theories of race and schooling. He is currently completing a book entitled *Schooling in Forbidden Fields: Carter G. Woodson and the Demands of Black Education* (forthcoming, Harvard University Press), which analyzes Carter G. Woodson's (1875–1950) critiques of the American school, the curricular materials he developed, and the ways ordinary teachers put his ideas into practice during Jim Crow. Extending from his past and emerging scholarship, Givens is interested in building bridges between the history of African American education and contemporary efforts to address challenges in public schooling. His new projects center on the recruitment and retention of African American teachers, working with practitioners to cultivate professional identities informed by the historical legacy of Black educators—their intellectual traditions and politically informed pedagogies.

Jerome Gourdine oversees the Manhood Development Program. Together with AAMA's leadership team, he recruits, supports, and develops MDP instructors. Gourdine regularly observes classes and provides feedback on performance. He designs and facilitates professional development seminars for MDP instructors and other administrators and teachers who want to deepen their engagement with African American male students. Prior to joining AAMA, for more than 20 years Gourdine served the Oakland

Unified School District as a teacher, assistant principal, and principal. Among his many accomplishments are the 2007 MetLife Principal of the Year Award, a distinguished title afforded to just 25 school leaders in the United States. Additionally, two of Gourdine's teachers were named California Teacher of the Year. Gourdine earned an MA in education and a secondary teaching credential in social science from the University of California, Berkeley. He also holds a secondary credential in social science from the California State University, Hayward, and a BS in political science from California State University, Long Beach.

Gregory Hodge is an organizational development and community-building consultant. He works with a range of groups from small nonprofits and foundations to public agencies, particularly school districts. He formerly served as the chief executive officer for California Tomorrow, an Oakland-based organization dedicated to building a strong multiracial and multicultural society that embraces diversity as our greatest asset. In addition, Gregory served as a member of the Oakland Unified School District Board of Education from 2000 to 2008. He previously served as the executive director of Safe Passages: The Oakland Child Health and Safety Initiative, and prior to that, he was the executive director of the Urban Strategies Council, where he also served as the director of a city-wide Youth Development Initiative, managed the Freedom Schools program, and worked as the regional representative of the Black Community Crusade for Children, an effort coordinated nationally by the Children's Defense Fund. He holds a bachelor of arts degree from Northwestern University and a law degree from Golden Gate University, San Francisco, CA.

Tyrone C. Howard is on the faculty in the Division of Urban Schooling in the Graduate School of Education & Information Studies at UCLA. He is the faculty director of Center X, the founder and director of the Black Male Institute, and an associate faculty member in the Bunche Center for African American studies at UCLA. Dr. Howard is the faculty associate director for the Academic Advancement Program at UCLA, which is the nation's premier student retention program for underrepresented students. He is the author of *Why Race and Culture Matter in Schools: Closing the Achievement Gap in America's Classrooms*, published by Teachers College Press. He has authored more than 50 peer-reviewed journal articles, book chapters, and other academic publications and reports. In 2007, Professor Howard received an Early Career Scholar award from the American Educational Research Association, the nation's premier educational research association. In 2007, Professor Howard received the UCLA GSE&IS Distinguished Teaching Award.

Jahi is a program manager for the Office of African American Male Achievement, where he recruits, supports, and develops Manhood Development Program instructors, observes classes, and provides feedback on performance. A musician and artist, he says that his community commitment informs his music, and in return his music motivates and inspires the community. Promoted from an MDP Lead Teacher, Jahi understands that children develop in an ecosystem. As an MDP teacher, it was crucial for him to engage all those who touch a student's life. From the school custodian to parents and teachers, Jahi created a community of care. He challenged the adults to see the beauty and brilliance of Black boys and to look beyond the episodic nature of a child's behavior. Jahi has worked with youth all over the globe and leads community efforts in support of Black boys throughout the Bay Area. Originally from Cleveland, now residing in Oakland, Jahi offers his style of music to microphones and speakers around the world with purpose, passion, and intellect. As an independent artist, sharing the same stages with musical legends such as Yasiin Bey, Blackalicious, Common, Talib Kweli, Public Enemy, and many more, Jahi creates opportunities for young people to be engaged, encouraged, and empowered academically and artistically.

Patrick Johnson is a student at the University of California, Berkeley, in the Graduate School of Education. His research explores how past Black media texts function in the lives of Black college students and contribute to their conceptions of Blackness. He is particularly interested in the ways that students who did not experience Black media texts in their original temporal context leverage past Black media to substantiate their conceptions of generational difference. Additionally, he investigates how participants' gendered positionalities from their readings inform their readings and memories of past Black media texts.

Maxine McKinney de Royston is a faculty member in Curriculum and Instruction at the University of Wisconsin, Madison. She received her PhD in education from the University of California, Berkeley. Dr. McKinney de Royston is committed to disrupting racialized inequities in education through her research and teaching on pedagogical approaches and characteristics of learning settings that seek to improve the educational outcomes and experiences of African American students. Her research focuses on the linkages between race, identity, and learning, with a focus on mathematics and science classrooms and predominantly African American learning environments. Dr. McKinney de Royston's current project is a comparative analysis of how schools and teachers in Oakland, CA, and in Pittsburgh, PA, conceptualize and respond to issues of race and poverty.

kihana miraya ross is an assistant professor of African American studies at Northwestern University. She holds a PhD in education from the University of California, Berkeley. Her program of research draws on critical ethnographic and participatory design methodologies to examine the multiplicity of ways that antiblackness is lived by Black students in what she calls the "afterlife of school segregation," a framework that illuminates the ways in which, despite the end of legal segregation of schooling, Black students remain systematically dehumanized and positioned as uneducable. Critically, her work also explores how Black educators and students collectively imagine and resist antiblackness and racialization processes more generally. Specifically, her conceptualization of Black educational fugitive space explores the ways Black students and educators enact educational fugitivity through the social production of Black space in the margin. She is particularly interested in the ways Black educational fugitive space manifests as both departure and refuge from the gratuitous violence of the afterlife of school segregation, and spawns the possibilities for rebirth and resistance.

Na'ilah Suad Nasir is the sixth president of the Spencer Foundation, which supports research about education. She is a professor of education and African American studies at the University of California, Berkeley, where she has served on the faculty since 2008. She also served as vice chancellor for equity and inclusion at UC Berkeley from 2015 to 2017. Nasir earned her PhD in educational psychology at UCLA in 2000, and was a member of the faculty in the School of Education at Stanford University from 2000 to 2008. Her work focuses on issues of race, culture, learning, and identity. She is the author of *Racialized Identities: Race and Achievement for African-American Youth*, and has published numerous scholarly articles. Nasir is a member of the National Academy of Education and a fellow of the American Educational Research Association (AERA). In 2016 she was the recipient of the AERA Division G Mentoring Award.

David Philoxene is a PhD student at the University of California, Berkeley, in the Graduate School of Education's Social & Cultural Studies Department, with almost 20 years of experience within the broader professional field. His work seeks to unpack the cumulativity of violence in urban socioecologies, particularly amongst youth of color, and highlight spaces of resilience. As an Oakland native, he has worked on local issues as classroom teacher, school design-team member, teacher supervisor, and researcher. He has been an NIH/NIGMS Predoctoral Fellow at University of California, San Francisco, examining violence as a public health issue, and a Chancellor's Fellow at UC Berkeley, with interdisciplinary work within public health, urban planning, and education. David has a BA in sociology and African American studies from UC Berkeley and a MEd and secondary teaching credential from UCLA.

Pedro A. Noguera is the distinguished professor of education at the Graduate School of Education and Information Studies and faculty director for the Center for the Transformation of Schools at UCLA. He is a sociologist whose scholarship and research focus on the ways in which schools are influenced by social and economic conditions as well as by demographic trends in local, regional, and global contexts. Dr. Noguera serves on the boards of numerous national and local organizations and appears as a regular commentator on educational issues on CNN, MSNBC, National Public Radio, and other national news outlets. From 2009 to 2012 he served as a trustee for the State University of New York (SUNY) as an appointee of the governor. In 2014 he was elected to the National Academy of Education. Dr. Noguera received his bachelor's degree in sociology and history and a teaching credential from Brown University in 1981 and earned his master's degree in sociology from Brown in 1982. He earned his doctorate in sociology from the University of California, Berkeley, in 1989. Dr. Noguera was a classroom teacher in public schools in Providence, RI, and Oakland, CA, and continues to work with schools nationally and internationally as a researcher and advisor. Dr. Noguera is the author of several books, including *City Schools and the American Dream* (Teachers College Press, 2003) and *Unfinished Business: Closing the Achievement Gap in Our Nation's Schools* (Jossey-Bass, 2006).

Sepehr Vakil is an assistant professor of learning sciences in the School of Education and Social Policy at Northwestern University. Previously he was assistant professor of STEM education and the associate director of equity and inclusion in the Center for STEM Education at the University of Texas at Austin. He holds a PhD in education from the University of California, Berkeley. Broadly, his research examines the politics of learning and identity in secondary and postsecondary engineering and computer science contexts. Dr. Vakil's teaching and research are informed by sociocultural, cultural-historical, and critical theories of learning, practice, and pedagogy. He recently received the National Academy of Education/Spencer Foundation Postdoctoral fellowship, where he will be investigating the cultural production of political identity among undergraduate engineering and computer science students of color. Working in partnership with communities and educators, Vakil also draws on design-based and participatory research methodologies to explore new transformative possibilities for STEM teaching and learning.

Index